Praise for See! Believe! Achieve!

Bob Grossi is more than a teacher, he is a prophet. In the best of biblical tradition prophets are sent not to speak to the future but to interpret the present. His reflections on the vocation of teaching are born out of his passion for making a difference, personal sacrifice, carrying his own cross with dignity, and sharing the burdens of others. I highly recommend this book as an invitation to a deeper understanding of the meaning of vocation and life. His good counsel has a professional wisdom and is animated by a deep understanding of the hungers of the human spirit. Bob Grossi is a teacher and a leader for yesterday, today and tomorrow.

—Monsignor Clement J. Connolly, Pastor
Holy Family Church South Pasadena, California

The wait is over... Finally a book that encompasses lesson planning and techniques, that will direct educators to a more efficient mapping of the curriculum that adheres to state standards. Bob Grossi has done just that. With creative suggestions, specific instructions and lessons for the whole year. A must buy!!! I mean it!

—Ron Beadle
Los Angeles County / Teacher of the Year 1995
San Gabriel Valley Consortium / Reading
Teacher of the Year 1995. Bassett Unified School
District Educator for thirty-three years. Currently
working in the Mountain View District / five years

Robert Grossi's passionate commitment to the success of his students for the past thirty-five years has earned him the love and respect of his students, their families as well as that of his fellow educators and administrators. His book lays the groundwork for encouraging excellent teacher practice which leads to greater achievement for students and teachers alike. Robert Grossi reminds us of the honor of being a teacher and how to facilitate our own practices toward the goal of excellence.

—Tanya T. Benzinger
Educator and Parent

"Mr. G" truly fostered a compelling sense of success in the classroom. His passion for teaching and road map to success provided his students with the empowering force to shine brightly. He saw the talents I had inside and enthusiastically encouraged me to achieve my greatest potential.

—Sabrina Sanchez

Mr. Grossi is a dear friend and former teacher of mine. Sabrina was inducted into the Alpha Kappa Delta (International Sociology Honors Society) and Phi Sigma Iota (International Foreign Language Honor Society). The National Dean's List 2001-2005 and published a sociology thesis.

SEE!
BELIEVE!
ACHIEVE!

To Lois —
Always Believe!

Robert Grossi

Robert Grossi

SEE!
BELIEVE!
ACHIEVE!

A book for discovering the
heart and soul of teaching

Tate Publishing & Enterprises

Published by Tate Publishing & Enterprises, LLC
127 E. Trade Center Terrace | Mustang, Oklahoma 73064 USA
1.888.361.9473 | www.tatepublishing.com

Tate Publishing is committed to excellence in the publishing industry. The company reflects the philosophy established by the founders, based on Psalm 68:11,
"The Lord gave the word and great was the company of those who published it."

Book design copyright © 2010 by Tate Publishing, LLC. All rights reserved.
Cover design by Kellie Southerland
Interior design by Blake Brasor

Published in the United States of America

ISBN: 978-1-61566-570-9
1. Education, Classroom Management
2. Education, Teaching Methods & Materials, General
2010.1.17

Acknowledgments

As I look back, I realize that there are many blessings of family, friends, parents, and students who have contributed to my personal growth as an educator. Thank you to everyone for sharing yourself, your friendship, gifts, ideas, and educational experiences with me over the years. Your presence in my life and encouragement led me to the completion of this book.

I would like to extend my appreciation and love for my wife, Marilyn, who was filled with enthusiasm and positive comments as she sat through my challenging times and many joyful moments in teaching. She always shared the beauty of each experience and what I could learn from all those educational moments. I love her, and she is a gift.

I am grateful to all the teachers, administrators, and schools who offered time and their expertise over the years and during visits to provide me with educational information.

My thanks to all the editors, proofreaders, and publishers for your guidance, direction, and critique of my manuscript.

Table of Contents

Author's Notes

Education is more than the imparting of information. In a deeper sense, it is the giving of oneself to another in the hope that the other (students) will grow and search for the real meaning of life in all of its beauty. You, as educators, have given of yourself in so many ways.

In the classroom you have taught your subject and life skills. You have seen each student as an individual. How wonderful you must feel in your accomplishments as an educator.

There were challenges along the way which made me stop, think, and discover more about myself and my role as an educator. Did I acknowledge the student's search for individuality along with knowledge? That was one of my goals, and it inspired me to grow as a teacher, thereby encouraging each student to realize more successes.

Learning more about ourselves as individuals and educators helps us understand that we have to be gentle with ourselves because change takes time. There have been many joys, and being the teacher and a learner provided possibilities to embark on new educational horizons. We as educators offer the basic tools that students need to face life, and then it is up to them to use what they learned. Awesome responsibility!

Both the teacher and student find that the process of learning has many beginnings, directions, and decisions. "Most of what we learn comes from the heart. The mind gives us direction, but the heart gives life meaning" (Cheerful Hearts). It has been a joy teaching and stretching a student's mind by helping each person as an individual to reach his or her full potential.

Our talents as educators should include assisting students and ourselves in being creative problem solvers and out-of-the-box thinkers, which in turns helps strengthen skills. Additionally, we have the talents within to offer skills for isolating problems, discovering areas of improvement, and finding positive solutions. So, let's use those motivational talents and create more accomplished thinkers.

It is my belief that an educator's mission is to be part of a team and do his or her part so that the school community will be a caring, enjoyable, and exciting learning environment. If students look forward to attending school, they will want to learn. Also, teachers and staff will carry out their responsibilities with joy and enthusiasm. I believe that is what school is all about.

It has been my pleasure to be in the educational profession for the last thirty-five years.

My many experiences include: in the classroom by teaching (grades 5–12 over the years), attending workshops, completing administrative duties as vice-principal and principal, giving educational in-services, consultant for administrators and schools, and sharing as an educational instructor (mentor program for University of San Francisco).

There is a need for educators to challenge their thinking, vision, decision-making, and strategic planning by regular self-evaluation of their classroom curriculum throughout the school year. Let us offer each other ideas to reflect on inner feelings and experiences as it connects to attitudes, planning tips, management programs, and instructional strategies for students in a "success-oriented" classroom environment.

This book is the completion of all that I have learned from teachers, students, administrators, attending workshops, reading books and articles, and managing classes as a teacher. Over thirty-five years, there have been few changes in the principles of education, but my understanding of them certainly has changed. The basics of education are the job of a classroom teacher. It is my hope that the information, ideas, and examples contained herein will confirm what you are already doing in your classroom and that you will be able to select a key point(s) to take and use in your lesson-planning, classroom, and with your students.

Foreword

As you read through the book, the first thing that will strike you is how much Bob Grossi loves teaching. Every word is carefully chosen and conveys a passion and intensity for education that every teacher and student should strive for in life. I can tell you that Bob is not only like this when it comes to teaching; he is passionate about everything in his life.

When you see him, he always has such a big smile on his face and is so eager to hear what you are up too, and it is not long before you are smiling. This man is a teacher through and through, not because he is always giving explanations or testing your knowledge; but because he listens, thinks about what you say, and shows you he cares.

I am not saying that this is all it takes to be a teacher. You obviously need to have other qualities like knowing your subject matter. How many times have you heard a student say about a teacher, "they know their material, they just don't know how to teach it to me." Bob refers to this openly in his book: being in tune with students, checking progress, adapting lessons and teaching styles to meet students' needs.

The proof of his willingness to listen and contemplate what you say, and really take it to heart, can be seen by the many testimonies from students and teachers he provides in his book. This book is a collection of not only Bob's own thoughts, but of what he has learned from students, teachers, workshops, and classes.

Bob acknowledges that there is no one "right" way to teach; everyone has to find the way that best suits them and their students. His many years of experience have left him with a wealth of information, and I think it is wonderful he has chosen to share it. Whether you have just started teaching or have been teaching for decades, his book will inspire you to think about your teaching, encourage you to look at things in a new way, and provide you with sound advice for lesson planning and classroom management.

—Lubi Lenaburg, PhD Education
Programs Evaluator UC Santa Barbara

Introduction

Challenge your journey with a road map of thoughts, attitudes, "tried and true" methods, materials, and teacher involvement tips for classroom planning. Reviewing student progress regularly throughout the school year enables you to appropriately pace instruction, ensures that all the achievement standards are adequately addressed, helps to acquire necessary resources, and gives you opportunities to meet the individual and group needs of students.

Is there a best way to teach? No! There are only alternatives whose effectiveness depends on the individual teacher's view of education, goals, and belief in student progress. The key word for students and teachers should be *success* as a person and student.

As educators, we must possess the enthusiasm and energy to see the invisible, believe the impossible, and achieve the incredible.

To be a star, you must shine your own light,
follow your own path, and don't worry
about the darkness, for that is when
Stars Shine Brightest!

(Hallmark–1989)

Congratulations, teachers and educators! You have proven to yourself and others that you have the ability to work closely with other teachers, administrators, and parents and to help children learn and be concerned with their problems. The demands of teaching are great: strategic planning, standards, administrators, parents, conferences, meetings, workshop attendance, and I could go on with the ongoing responsibilities of our profession. But through it all, you continue to withstand stress and demonstrate an idealism and success-oriented view of the work we must complete in the name of children and their education.

See the invisible! Yes, I am speaking to you as an educator. It is time to celebrate your past accomplishments that are visible to you and others. Stop and reflect on these questions! Are you continuing to allow yourself the freedom to challenge your thinking in planning? What is your vision of the classroom environment and student progress? There will be these questions, other positive challenges to face, and changes to make as a teacher; it is up to you to accept them. The key to planning and an active-learning atmosphere involves educators and students being able to examine the educational process and turn opportunities into successes.

Part One

What is Your Road Map for the School Year?

Introduction

I found this passage by Nancye Sims (author of books, poetry, and greeting cards). It is a statement of courage, respect for life, and a willingness to know and accept yourself first before reaching out to others. There is a fragile thread that binds us to one another.

> Don't dismiss your dreams! To be without dreams is to be without hope. To be without hope is to be without purpose.
>
> Don't be afraid to encounter challenges. It is in taking chances that we learn how to be brave and grow as our own person.
>
> Don't run through life so fast that you forget where you have been, where you are going and do not forget those people who have entered your life in a positive way.

My book speaks about the 'heart and soul' of teaching, not just planning tips, thinking, procedures, classroom management, and other educational topics. Teachers, you and your students are making connections as a "family" with signs of growth personally and academically. Hope! Dream! Take each instructional day as a gift for you and your students to encounter the beauty of challenge and rewards of successes.

Teachers and educators, you are commended on your ability to prepare, plan, and implement a classroom curriculum and environment where concepts and ideas are placed into action. Your vision, mission, goals, objectives, and philosophies offer students new possibilities to be involved in learning.

May you find strength and courage to face the position of a teacher with its many complex duties, interruptions, demands, administrative requests, parent concerns, changing roles, instructors, mediators, counselors, caregivers, peacemakers and much more.

We have the "power" as teachers to bring out the beauty of knowledge and understanding of a child's own uniqueness to the forefront. When we as teachers provide an open environment for a child or our students to be aware of their individual gifts, the successes benefit everyone.

Yes, teaching is demanding, but as educators we should feel a sense of responsibility and satisfaction to lead children to real-life discoveries.

Letters were written to me by former students at the end of a school year, and I would like to share them as examples of the heart and soul of education. First, letters included in this book serve as direct examples of what I have learned from my students. Second, other names will be used in place of actual student names. Third, permission was given by each student to use their letters for publication.

Dear Mr. Grossi,
Thank you for the wonderful years we have spent together. You have been more than a teacher to me; you have been a friend. Your courage and passion for life has inspired me, and helped me to try

new things. I will take everything you have taught me and apply to my high school life. You will never be forgotten or left behind, for you hold the gift of sharing knowledge.

Love,
—Elizabeth Smith
(eighth grade student)

Reflections: The reinforcement of qualities like enthusiasm, concentrating on the individuality of each student, and knowledge offered in real-life situations are important goals to be considered for each lesson plan.

Dear Mr. Grossi,

Thank you for all you have done for me. You have helped me at times when I was struggling, you encouraged me to do better, and you helped me make my life easier.

Thank you,
—Mark Jones
(sixth grade student)

Reflections: The emphasis on the importance of patience, listening, and the bond between a teacher and student must be reinforced throughout the school year.

Dear Mr. Grossi,

Thank you for everything! You showed us how to work together as a group. You wouldn't stop until we were successful and learned everything we needed to know. We have achieved so many things, and especially how to connect with one another through all the problems. Thanks for all your help; we have finally grown up.

Love,
—Melissa Sanchez
(eighth grade student)

Reflections: Peacemaking talents and the realization that helping students with conflict/resolution techniques during difficult times is as important for life as academic skills.

It is time for me to challenge your teaching journey with a road map of thoughts, attitudes, "tried and true" methods, materials, and teacher involvement tips for classroom planning. Be encouraged to review student progress regularly throughout the school year, and that will enable you to pace instruction, ensure consistent skill development, address achievement standards, help acquire necessary materials, and give you opportunities to meet the individual and group needs of your students.

Watch out for the dangers of side roads or "quick fixes" in thinking and overall planning for your classroom curriculum. The benefits of organization and good decision-making will produce a logical vision, clear goals and objectives, reachable instructional outcomes, and valid assessment results.

● ● ● ● ● ● ● ● ● ● ● ● ●

The Violinist

Once there was a violinist who played in an enormous symphony orchestra. There was nothing he loved better than hearing the beautiful sounds of the orchestra's music. But the man was discouraged and felt very insignificant in the midst of so many instruments. What difference does it make if I play or not? he thought. No one could possibly hear my single violin among all the other great musicians in the orchestra.

Then one day, the violinist missed rehearsal. The conductor called him aside the next day and said, "We missed you yesterday. Something didn't sound right when the orchestra began, and it was then that I noticed you were gone. You play so beautifully, and I want you to know it's truly a pleasure to have you in the orchestra."

The violinist was astounded. "Do you mean that you can distinguish my instrument from all the others?"

"Of course," the conductor answered him. "How else would I be able to advise each musician to play louder or softer, slower or faster?"

—Anonymous author

This story is a testament to the importance of each child, teacher, and adult. It is incredible how we are intertwined and contribute to one another's successes or problems. There are no chance encounters, only orchestrated accounts of how we communicate, develop, and create possibilities for one another. This account of "The Violinist" is a statement of the "specialness" that each person brings to our lives. Let us begin our expedition and investigation with our road map to thinking, organization, decision-making, planning, and assessment.

Challenge Your Teaching Journey: Pre-Planning Considerations

Take the time to read and reflect on this meaningful message. The connections made as the teacher discovers the talents within each child is a gift in itself for successes in student learning. As a teacher, you are a gift. Each student is a gift. Be alert to look inside the wrappings and note the uniqueness of each person as you prepare your vision and strategic planning considerations.

Persons as Gifts

Persons are gifts which are sent to each other. Some are wrapped very beautifully; they are very attractive when you first see them. Some come in very ordinary wrapping paper. Others have been mishandled in the mail. Once in a while there is a "Special Delivery." Some persons are gifts which are very loosely wrapped, others very tightly.

But the wrapping is not the gift; it is sad to make that mistake. Sometimes the gift is very easy to open up. Sometimes you need help; it is challenging.

Have I ever really looked inside the wrappings? Afraid to? Perhaps I need to accept the gift that I am, as well as other persons. I am a gift to other persons. Open the gift and see the beauty within. Every meeting of persons is an exchange of gifts.

—Anonymous author

Introduction

The road map to a teacher's journey in thinking and planning must begin with clear vision and mission statements. The collaboration of teachers and students to formulate these statements will result in their commitment to positive-learning outcomes throughout the year. As educators, we need to consistently discover the essential connections between vision, mission, goals, objectives, curriculum, instruction, and assessment. The journey toward collaboration involves a vision and mission that is clear, entails the formulation and articulation of goals, and agreed upon by the teacher and students.

Consider these questions to reflect on pre-planning thinking about learning strategies, skill development, and student involvement in the learning process. Are teachers and students:

1. Offered a sense of direction for planning and learning?
2. Included in the forming of these beliefs?
3. Allowed to build attitudes and skills to accomplish these tasks?
4. Committed to building a greater collaboration?
5. Resolving difficulties, conflicts, and celebrating successes?
6. Does the teacher recognize student gifts, individuality, and needs?

Teachers and educators, let us honor your present and past successes and accomplishments. Yes, I am talking to you as an educator. Stop and reflect on these two questions: Are you continuing to allow yourself the freedom to challenge your thinking in planning? What is your vision of the classroom environment and student progress? There will be these questions and others for reflection, challenges to face, and changes to make as a teacher during your years as an educator. It is up to you to accept them. The key to planning and an active-learning atmosphere involves educators and students being able to examine the educational process and turn opportunities into successes.

Let us explore the core values of preplanning considerations: vision, mission, goals and objectives, philosophy, and outcomes. What are they? Why are they important? There will be samples and examples to offer you a new way of thinking for strategic planning. These belief values have been part of educational and school planning for a long time. It is my hope if an idea or concept "grabs your fancy" or you see a concept in a new light; you will take it and make it your own.

Step One: Vision Statements

Whether you are a classroom teacher considering long-range plans, a school, the district, or a business, the process of strategic planning begins with a vision as the first component of pre-planning. A vision statement is similar to a "picture" of your classroom or school curriculum and should remind you of what you are trying to build as an educational program and how you will involve students in the learning process.

A collaborative approach to building a collective vision is a source of motivation for both the teacher or administration, staff, and students to reinforce the sense of shared responsibility for student learning. Let us explore questions and ideas for establishing a clear vision direction.

• • • • • • • • • • • • •

Questions to reflect on creating a vision:

1. Are beliefs, philosophy, and school environment used as sources for planning?
2. What do you want to see in the future for your classroom and school curriculum?
3. Will you be positive, enthusiastic, and open to ideas?
4. Is your vision flexible to accommodate changes, methods, and new techniques?

Important beliefs for your vision:

1. Have clear organizational goals, objectives, missions, philosophies, and values.
2. Be specific and practical with your vision.
3. Post your expected outcomes for the year.
4. Involve all students and teachers in the process of active teaching and learning.
5. Realize that all beliefs and considerations are important for strategic planning.

Benefits of vision (You will notice successful results for students with these benefits):
1. Provides direction, purpose, consistency, and effective planning.
2. Promotes interest, commitment, and need for changes.

3. Encourages openness to creative solutions.
4. Builds confidence, loyalty, and ownership.

Vision killers (Your vision and student achievement will not occur immediately):

1. Tradition and "naysayers."
2. Fear of ridicule, complacency, and fatigued leaders.
3. Lack of motivation begins when there is too much discussion on vision.
4. Those who were left out of the planning process will not be enthusiastic.
5. The vision must include student-learning goals.

Congratulations! Imagine that it is five years from today's date and you, marvelously enough, created your most desirable classroom curriculum, school, or district vision. Now it is your job, as a teacher, staff or team, to describe and see if it is realistically around you." Vision statements should describe the best outcome possible, inspire people, and communicate the direction of the curriculum and programs. It needs to be short enough that people can remember it and draw people into the message. Some vision examples:

Number one: Pinecrest Elementary School
    "The mission of our school is development of what our school will 'look like' five years from now, or our dream of a 'perfect' Pinecrest."

Vision: To develop a community that:

1. Embraces knowledge and learning as a means to personal growth and fulfillment.
2. Values itself and others.
3. Accepts that each of us is personally and collectively responsible for maximizing our potential.

Pinecrest Elementary School
313 South 9ᵗʰ St. Immoklee, FL 34142
377–8000 Fax: 377–8001

Number two: Pond Union Elementary School District

"The district will provide a quality education, providing the basis for students to become lifelong learners as well as moral, ethical, and compassionate people. A partnership of staff, students, parents, and community will prepare students to be responsible citizens and productive members of the communities in which they live."

Pond Union Elementary School District
29585 Pond Rd., Pond, CA 93280
Fax: 661–792–2303

Number three: Teacher and Librarian

"As a Teacher and Librarian, I will be actively involved in the teaching process, promoting and teaching literacy standards to all grades in all curricular areas. The ultimate goal is to ensure the continued use of the library for reading and education of all students."

—Michael Walsh, Benton Schools

Number four: Dr. Thomas L. Higdon Elememtary School

"The staff at Dr. Higdon Elementary will use best practices in instruction and technology, encourage student responsibility and a safe, engaging environment in which students will be able to achieve their highest potential."

Number five: Pendleton High School

"Pendleton High School will provide a safe, respectful, and inviting educational environment through:

- Positive interaction between staff and students.
- Continuous technology updates.
- Academic rigor and relevance.
- Appropriate student to teacher ratio.
- Consistent policies of attendance and discipline."

In order to accomplish these vision statements Pendleton High School will:

- Continuously and consciously strive to pursue our vision.
- Make all decisions based on what is best for students and their education.
- Value staff participation in the decision making process.

(Samples, there are more statements)

Pendleton High School
1800 NW Carden Ave.
Pendleton, OR 97801
541-966-3800 Fax: 541-966-3813

Number six: Prescott Unified School District

The Smart Choice

"Our vision is to be the most innovative, effective, and respected educational organization in the Prescott area by fulfilling public trust."

"Because school must provide experiences which help students to lead lives that are personally satisfying, healthy, and supportive of the society in which they live,"

They then list 10 "belief" statements; an example follows.

"We believe there is a critical need for students to learn how to think, understand concepts, and apply what they learned."

Prescott Unified School District
146 S. Granite St., Prescott, AZ 86303
928-445-5400 Fax: 928-445-7766

● ● ● ● ● ● ● ● ● ● ● ● ●

Step Two: Mission Statement

Vision and mission statements are related to each other by focusing your thinking, enthusiasm, and decisions toward educational goals and objectives that are important to you. This will energize strong support from educational and community stakeholders and provide teachers and schools with ideal outcomes to reach in the future. Mission statements represent actions and instructions that will promote current classroom experiences to help you arrive at your destination.

The mission statement is a guide for direction and decision-making by the teacher and everyone connected with the school. All curriculum programs, development, planning, management, and activities are under the guidance of the mission, and there is a shared responsibility of teachers, administrators, board members, students, and parents. It is important that teachers and community build a collective vision and mission statement together that is clear, compelling, and connected to teaching and learning outcomes. A mission statement is foundational and states the purpose of the school's existence. It answers the question, "Why do we do what we do?" A mission statement begins with clear beliefs, builds on them, defines who you are, and becomes a statement of purpose.

Mission Statement Model

Vision and Mission Statements
Goals, Objectives, Outcomes
Strategies and Criteria
Organization, Making Decisions, Staffing, Responsibilities
Training, Materials, Tools
Assessment

Mission Statement Examples
Number one: Foothill Elementary School

"In an ever-changing community, Foothill Elementary School has a vision that ensures a safe, nurturing, and flexible environment in which each student can attain academic success through the collaboration and commitment of our students, teachers, parents and community."

> Foothill Elementary School
> Monterey Peninsula Unified School District
> 700 Pacific, Monterey, CA 93940
> 831–649–1200

Number two: Newport Mill Middle School

"As a diverse community of learners at Newport Mills Middle School, our mission is to work cooperatively to create a positive learning environment. To achieve this mission, we will work together to analyze our strengths and needs to take responsibility for our actions and to be models of motivated, lifelong learners."

> Newport Mills Middle School
> 11311 Newport Mills Rd.
> Kensington, MD 20895

Number three: Westlake High School

"Our mission is to empower students to become independent, lifelong learners. Our mission is 'Westlake High School … Where Excellence is Deliberate.'"

> Westlake High School
> 2370 Union Rd. SW
> Atlanta, GA 30331
> 404–345–5400

Number four: Morgan Hill Unified School District

"The mission of the Morgan Hill Unified School

District, serving a diverse community, is to create in students a passion for learning, and achievement through innovative, dynamic partnerships, and exceptional programs and support services.

> Morgan Hill Unified School District
> 15600 Concord Circle
> Morgan Hill, CA 95037
> 408–201–6000

• • • • • • • • • • • • •

Step Three: Goals and Objectives

Goals are broad statements emphasizing where you are and what skills and concepts will be taught. A collaborative approach to creating realistic goals by teachers and students offers more positive attention on classroom expectations. Objectives are specific, short-term, measurable, and observable behaviors for student successes.

Examples of Goals and Objectives:

Goal one: Students will gain a better understanding of the use of verbs in writing.

Objectives:

1. Review kinds of verbs and apply them in sentence and descriptive writing.
2. Identify how to use active and passive voice correctly in sentences.

3. Learn and practice the use of subject-verb agreement in sentence writing.

Goal two: Students will have a greater appreciation of respect as a value that would affirm dignity.

Objectives:

1. Read and discuss biographies that illustrate responses of respect toward others.
2. Write about a biographer as if you were telling the account to a younger child.
3. Discuss and witness how these people represent this in their lives.

   a. A family member who demonstrates respect for good health.
   b. A neighbor who demonstrates respect for children.
   c. A community member who demonstrates respect for community property.

Goal three: Students will understand short story elements for "Rain, Rain, Go Away" by Isaac Asimov.

Objectives:

1. Read the story and discuss the five reading strategies to determine the main points.
2. Discuss the elements of a short story after reading "Rain, Rain, Go Away": characters, conflicts, resolutions, setting, and plot.

3. Discuss the conflicts in this story as a class or in small groups:
   a. How can curiosity cause conflict?
   b. What types of conflicts can develop between people?
   c. How can one person have a conflict within him or her?

Goal four: Prepare, memorize, and know how to spell the words and write them in sentences from Unit 6.

Goal five: Students will memorize and recite "A Red, Red Rose" by Robert Burns.
(Sometimes goals can be the same as objectives.)

That is why objectives are formed to evaluate if the goal achieved is specific, measurable, and observable within student behaviors. We want to determine if we have or have not achieved our teaching instructional goal and students are able to obtain mastery. As a teacher, you want to think of objectives as key concepts for expanding lessons, making adjustments, and planning alternate assignments and assessments that will meet your short and long-range planning goals.

There are various names for objectives: learning outcomes, behavioral objectives, and measurable objectives. Regardless of the terminology, you want to know if the student either has or has not accomplished the objectives.

Goals:

1. How should the goal be accomplished?
2. What is the purpose of this goal?

Objectives:

1. Who are your students? What are the pre-requisites? What are the levels of students' prior knowledge?
2. What is the time frame for accomplishing this objective?
3. What information, conditions, and directions will students be given to accomplish the objective?
4. What are the criteria for acceptable performance?
5. How well do you want students to master the skill or concept?

Be aware of these pitfalls for setting goals:

1. Too numerous
2. Too broad
3. Too trivial
4. Too ambitious
5. Too unrealistic

I have used this student goal-setting form, "To Be the Best That I Can Be," for the last twenty years of teaching with marvelous results. There were a variety of forms investigated and used prior to adapting this form for myself, students, and their particular needs. I have found in my experiences that students respond in a more positive manner to simple and clear goal form. Primary teachers, you would have to adopt a simpler version. Teachers in grades five to eight, this form has been successful for my students. High school teachers, this format could be expanded into a more challenging tool for student assessment and self-evaluation.

1. Students receive goal forms at the beginning of each quarter.
2. Students are given directions on how to complete forms and assess progress.
3. Students are regularly directed on checking academic folders and goal forms correctly.
4. Student conferences are scheduled once a quarter.
5. Students write a self-evaluation once a quarter to check academic and goal successes.
6. Conference notes, self-evaluations, and goal forms are placed in each student's academic folders or portfolios.

To Be the Best That I Can Be
(Please Print)

_____

Last Name   First Name

During the first trimester, I want to be proud at being successful in the following areas in school:

Section 1–Academic Subjects
(select one or two academic goals only)

____Other	____Literature	____Grammar
____Vocabulary	____Handwriting	____CreativeWriting
____Math	____Social Studies	____Science

Check two or three areas that will help you to improve on your academic goals, or write in the active ways you will accomplish these goals.

____Listen better	____Follow Directions better
____Concentrate more	____Work better in groups
____Be better organized	____Write neater and clearer
____Complete quality work	____Use my time more wisely
____Improve on my study habits	____Ask more questions when needed
____Study for tests ahead of time	____Plan ahead-completing assignments

Other:

_____

_____

Section 2–Action Goals

Goal #1 - I would like to

_____

_____

by

_____

Goal #2–I would like to

_____

_____

by

_____

Section 3

I will work at my goals consistently and carefully as possible so that I may realize my continued progress. I will evaluate my successes and needs for improvement every six weeks with Mr. Grossi's guidance.

_____

Student Signature   Date

Step Four: Teaching Philosophy

One definition of the word *philosophy* from the dictionary states, "A set of ideas or beliefs relating to a particular field or activity." Education and teaching are all about enthusiasm and encouraging a positive attitude for student successes and lifelong learning. A teacher's philosophy is an ongoing process and evolves over the course of your career.

Teaching and schools are all about having a positive attitude for life, learning, and interacting with others: students, parents, community, teachers, and educators. The classroom atmosphere is critical to an organized and functional environment for student learning. It is impossible for teachers to know everything, but being flexible and willing to search for answers will strengthen content mastery. Two-way communication, offering a variety of teaching styles, realizing every student is different, involving students in learning, and a success-oriented approach all contribute to an educational philosophy.

I reflect on the years I have taught and know how much I have learned from my students as well as other teachers. Also, I realize their contributions have influenced my vision, mission, goals, and especially philosophy, and myself to realize that these values are flexible, "breathing," and "working" documents.

The demands of teaching and difficulties of working with many groups, requirements, and assessments are real and sometimes offer challenges to an educator's philosophy. It was my hope during my teaching years that students were comfortable with my classroom environment. The importance of a successful self-image, being able to respect one another, and looking forward to school are concepts of learning beyond content, skills, and subject matter. When you take the time to reflect on your own personal beliefs, it is my hope that these thoughts will inspire you to focus on the person first, then the student. Two possible philosophy samples follow. There are as many styles of individual philosophy statements as there are teachers. Remember, your statements should be flexible, and however short, long, or detailed they are depends upon the individual teacher.

● ● ● ● ● ● ● ● ● ● ● ● ● ●

Philosophy Statement Sample One
(Lynne, teacher friend):

Each student is a unique individual who needs a safe, secure, and simulating environment to discover who they are personally and academically. It will be one of my goals to develop the potential within to help them believe they are capable individuals. I have high and reasonable expectations and will do all that is possible to involve students in learning, realize their progress, and feel a sense of accomplishment. In addition, I will be emphasizing these areas for student successes:

1. I will encourage respect for themselves and others, responsibility, trust, and honesty.
2. I will reinforce good study skills and time management.
3. I will strengthen within them a love and motivation for learning.
4. I will help students accept challenges and learning experiences as opportunities for growth.
5. I will assist students in their development as lifelong learners.

6. I will provide experiences for growth in self-discipline and self-responsibility.

Teaching is a lifelong learning process with changing plans, philosophies, and new strategies. Remember that all students do not work or learn at the same rate, and knowing each child's strengths and weaknesses is a boost to his or her growth and self-esteem. As teachers, students, and parents, it is clear we need to work together toward an optimum educational experience and develop mutual goals for each student's future success.

• • • • • • • • • • • • •

Philosophy Statement Sample Two
(Robert Grossi):

I want to provide a positive learning environment and experiences for each student which combines respect, honesty, moral values, a belief in themselves, and instruction in the basics to develop the individual's lifelong skills. My goals and objectives will be focused on strengthening, encouraging, and creating an atmosphere that promotes these operating principles and academic success goals.

Operating Principles

1. To demonstrate respect and positive attitudes for all students and one another.
2. To enable all students to be all they can be.
3. To encourage all students to set up and achieve their goals.

Academic and Social Success

1. Assume an attitude of 100-percent responsibility.
2. Identify your strengths and work on your needs for improvement.
3. Set goals and objectives.
4. Take action and "just do it."
5. Persevere.

Be realistic. Demand the impossible.
There is a theory in education called TESA
Teacher expectation. Student achievement.
Interpretation: Whatever you expect—
you will get it!

Step Five: Outcome-Based Instructional Planning

These are reflections for teachers to assess for strategic planning and outcome-based instruction. There should be specific norms for a community of learners: mutual respect,respectful listening, participation and contribution by each member, and responsibility for one's own learning, as well as others.

The individual short and long-range planning program provides a teacher with opportunities to review actual curriculum and what goes on as practiced in the classroom. Standards, goals, objectives, scope and sequence, supplementary materials, assessment, conferences, and more are important indicators of exit outcome-based planning.

1. Implement instructional outcomes for each subject to match the actual curriculum.
2. Plan topics and subtopics with standards and scope and sequence.
3. Compare instructional time with curriculum expectations.
4. Evaluate assessment techniques and content with how it matches outcomes, goals, and objectives.
5. Realize that this approach can be used with all styles of plans: daily, weekly, short-term, long-range, and school-overview planning.

What do you want your students to know, understand, and be able to do? Ask this question about student progress and outcomes consistently. We need to consistently discover the essential connections between curriculum, instruction, and assessment. Grant Wiggins suggestions:

1. Construct meaning
2. Think and reason
3. Make connections
4. Solve problems
5. Communicate effectively
6. Be creative
7. Be productive, participate, and contribute

Grant Wiggins, "Re-Thinking Assessment: Performance Tasks and Criteria," UC Irvine Presentation 1991.

Basic skills to learn for the twenty-first century:

1. Basic skills:
   Reading, writing, new computation literacy skills, mathematics; if a student does not own a skill, it is not learned.
2. Thinking:
   Problem-solving, creative skills, use of imagination.
3. Computers:
   Giving dictation to computers.
4. Generalizing:
   Help students apply what they know.
5. Listening:
   Speaking and listening skills.

6. Fine Arts:
   Fine Arts classes tend to make students more successful.
7. Cooperation:
   Work collaboratively, contribute more, and managing and resolving conflicts.
8. Leadership Skills:
   Leading and following directions.
9. Management Skills:
   Self-awareness, self-knowledge, self-responsibility

Planning begins at learner outcomes.

Instruction (The "How")
    Teaching
    Strategies
    Processes
    Skills
    Coaching
    Facilitating

Curriculum (The "What")
    Knowledge
    Concepts

Learner Outcomes
    What all students should know, understand, and be able to do.

Supporting Outcomes
    What student should know, understand, and be able to do by the end of this year or subject that supports the learner outcomes.

Assessment begins after instruction.

• • • • • • • • • • • • • •

Outcome-base lesson plan terminology

1. Learner Outcome: These outcomes are planned for all students when they complete elementary, middle school, or high school. What students should know, understand, and be able to do.
2. Supporting Outcome (s): These are learn-

ing results that are expected of all students in "what they should know, understand, and be able to do" in a specific subject or by the end of the year.

3. Indicator of an Outcome (s): These are observable and assessable behaviors from the accomplishments, feedback, and needs of students.

4. Outcomes are Expected Results:
   1. Vision, Mission, Goals + Targets = Provides direction
   2. Objectives + Small segments = Action taken
   3. Outcomes + Finished products = Completed by all students

Marilyn Tabor, "Portfolio and Authentic Assessment" workshop, Irvine Unified School District, 1994.

Teacher Goal Setting Form

_____
School Year

Teacher: _____ Date: _____

Vision Statement (Teacher or School)

_____
_____
_____

Mission Statement (Teacher or School)

_____
_____
_____

Goal Categories

1. Professional development and Improvement
2. Curriculum and classroom instruction
3. Technology and integration
4. Classroom management
5. Classroom environment and atmosphere
6. Student progress academically and personally

Goals for the school year. (Select no more than 5 goals.)

1. _____

2. _____

3. _____

4. _____

5. _____

Objectives

1. _____

2. _____

3. _____

4. _____

5. _____

Philosophy (Teacher or Subject)

1. _____

2. _____

3. _____

4. _____

5. _____

Outcomes ("What students should know, be able to do, and understand.")

1. _____

   Subject   When

2. _____

3. _____

4. _____

5. _____

Decisions, Decisions:
Organization and Decision-Making

Ever feel like a frog? Frogs feel slow, ugly, puffy, drooped, and tired. The frog feeling comes when you want to be together and bright but feel dull. You want to share but are selfish. You want to be thankful but feel "cranky." You want to be big and are small. You want to care but are indifferent. Yes, at one time or another, each of us has found himself or herself on the lily pad floating down the river of life. Tired, frightened, disgusted and discouraged, but too froggish to budge.

The Frog and Beautiful Young Maiden

A Fairy Tale

Once upon a time there was a frog. But he wasn't really a frog. He was prince who had all this potential, but looked and felt like a frog. A wicked witch had cast a spell on him. Only a kiss of a beautiful young maiden could save him. Wait a minute, when do cute chicks kiss frogs? So there he sat—unkissed prince in frog form. But miracles do happen! One day a beautiful maiden grabbed him up and gave him a big smack. *Crash! Boom! Zap!* There he was—a handsome prince. And you know the rest. They lived happily ever after.

—Wes Seelinger

So what is the task of teachers and schools? To kiss frogs, of course! What a tremendous gift and a challenge you have to unleash the potential in a child.

What is your vision and mission? Your short and long-range plans should incorporate your expectations and vision, goals, objectives, and mission that relate to the vision of your school.

Is the classroom environment free to discern the gifts of each person? The safe, caring, and consistent classroom atmosphere will create successes for your students. Are there methods to share and clarify vision and gifts? Is there a way to deal with conflicts? A consistent and well thought out classroom management program will reinforce the success of your vision, mission, and educational goals.

Do you include lifelong guidelines in your attitude, thinking, and planning for your classroom curriculum to motivate students? You have to answer these questions for yourself.

Introduction

Even with good planning and vision, real problems with a few and ordinary mischief will occur. Organization is a matter of decision-making, and teachers must prepare in thought, attitude, planning, and environment to create success stories for students. A classroom that values commitment will encourage students to keep their word, keep trying until their goal is reached, and follow through on developing the qualities of respect, responsibility, and compassion.

Teachers and administrators, challenge your thinking, motivate a collaborative vision, provide opportunities for action, model and lead the way, encourage more success stories. Yes, you can see the invisible. Are you ready to believe the impossible?

Freedom, Wisdom, and Good Thinking

Kenneth Sollitt explains (*Character Education–Year 2*, chapter on freedom by John Heidel and Marion Lyman-Mersereau, 1999), "Freedom is the opportunity to make decisions. The individual person has the ability to make right decisions. It can be achieved only in a climate of freedom, and no one learns to make right decisions without being free to make wrong ones."

If we tap into the principles of freedom and allow ourselves to make mistakes, we are challenging ourselves and students to embrace different thinking, options, and viewpoints. Freedom is a key tool for educators to understand and correct mistakes because that is when learning occurs. When we give students the freedom and assurance that mistakes are lessons, then we have given them the greatest gift.

● ● ● ● ● ● ● ● ● ● ● ● ●

Good Teaching and Good Thinking

1. Having passion, reason, and motivation.
2. Realizing students are consumers of knowledge.
3. Being able to listen, question, and remember that each student and class is different.

4. Being flexible, experiment, and adjusting to changes.
5. Possessing a sense of humor.
6. Offering caring and nurturing when necessary.
7. Developing individual minds and their talents.
8. Supporting visionary leadership and strength of character.
9. Mentoring students individually and as team members.

Good Planning and Good Thinking

1. Be broad and adventurous.
2. Create an atmosphere of wondering, problem finding, and investigating.
3. Build explanations and understandings.
4. Make plans and be strategic.
5. Be intellectually careful.
6. Seek and evaluate reasons.

"Teaching Thinking and Preparing for Student Learning," South Pasadena Unified School District, in-service for teachers, administrators, and paraprofessionals.

Wisdom and freedom provide a clear path for sound decisions, organization, and quality lesson planning. Teaching and education is an ongoing process of assessment, development, and adjustments. A teacher as an organizer has the ability to offer students an effective classroom atmosphere of wonder, problem-solving, and investigating. He or she organizes learning and works primarily with the similarities and differences in children. The main task and responsibility is to create an environment, lessons, and activities which children are able to achieve and be successful.

> Wisdom is the insight that uproots all delusion. Wisdom is more than intelligence, more than the common sense to act appropriately in life situations. Wisdom means seeing directly into the true nature of things.
>
> -Buddhist text

Good Organizer

What are some characteristics of a teacher who is a good organizer. A good organizer...

1. Provides guidance, leadership, and invites others into the decision-making process.
2. Helps students and teachers to clarify their own vision, goals, and objectives.
3. Delegates and distributes duties and encourages students to keep on task.
4. Emphasizes strengths, progress, and achievement.
5. Guides students and teachers in regular assessment and self-evaluation.
6. Maintains a common purpose.

These are definitely key qualities of any good organizer and of a first-rate teacher. The demands of teaching today are many, but teachers continue their strong efforts to make clear decisions and organize consistent teaching programs. Organization plus decision-making plus authentic assessment equals student progress and achievement.

There is a saying you probably know: "If you fail to plan," or, "You plan to fail." This saying would describe anyone who shows lack of preparation, problems, and poor follow-through on lesson plan goals and objectives. Good decision-making, organization, wisdom, and freedom of thought are tools for solid strategic planning. Three good planning practices:

1. A teacher needs to write down lessons, skills taught, and projects.
2. A teacher must identify all lessons and projects to prioritize and plan completion time.
3. A teacher should organize and plan to discover the preparation time required.

Time management is key to an effective approach to completion of classroom skill learning, projects, and development of an interactive learning environment. Time management is a quality concept for both the teacher and students to work on a schedule for completion of all lessons. Avoid side roads to inconsistent organizational plans and use of time.

Dear Mr. Grossi,

Thanks for everything you've taught me through the last three years. You've helped me grow and express myself through writing and working on a positive attitude. You have also helped me understand the importance of time management and I have renewed my learning for direct objects, kinds of verbs; introductory, body and concluding paragraphs. You must be the Grammar King. I am very happy you were my teacher. I'll never forget you or the good times and memories we had in class. For example, the hilarious jokes or clever comebacks made learning real and interesting. I did enjoy doing the plays and other programs. Thanks for making this year a great one!

Sincerely,
—Gabriella Rivera
(tenth grade student)

Reflections: The eagerness that your students show for learning and being involved in the "life" of school is your enthusiasm, planning, and creating a success oriented classroom environment. Don't forget the importance of listening, organizing and managing time, and the gift of humor.

Parent Assistance and Volunteers

Everyone knows the comprehensive tasks teachers must complete with the constant planning, organization, decision-making, daily instruction, and answering to a variety of people. "On the other side of the coin" there are many positive experiences for teachers, especially student successes, cooperation, and support from fellow educators, and this makes our profession a challenging and ever-changing profession.

Most teachers are thankful for volunteers and parents who are able to assist in many ways in the classroom. They can be a tremendous help or a concern depending on training and a professional approach to these key areas.

Communication

A survey or letter sent home, a personal telephone call, or scheduling a meeting at the beginning of the school year are main ways to secure parents. You could also be assigned a volunteer, or there is an established person who volunteers in a particular grade level. Be very specific regarding job duties, expectations, procedures, and checking in and out. I have found a survey sent home, followed by a telephone call and interview to be a smoother process.

Organization

Once you have accepted your parent volunteer, consider the following: be aware of their talents and experience, share classroom procedures, and let them know what to do and where things are in the classroom. It is time to make a schedule and post it, send it home, or print a weekly newsletter. Remember, a parent and volunteer's time and efforts are valuable and they want to help you and your students.

Instruction

It is necessary that those working with you are aware of how to use instructional methods when asked to help students. These are some possible areas in which you may take advantage of helpers: math, reading, writing, students who are experiencing difficulty with specific skills or subjects. If you do use a volunteer or parent for instruction, check progress regularly, how they work with students, make certain the volunteer knows the curriculum and basic teaching techniques, and confidentiality is important.

Suggestions for volunteers:

1. Reading with small groups or individuals.
2. Help students with make-up work.
3. Work with students who need remedial work.
4. Check students as they complete assignments.
5. Check homework.
6. Help with projects.
7. Monitor students at centers and the computer.
8. Help with bulletin boards, copying, restocking classroom materials, etc.

It has been my pleasure to have parents, volunteers, and teaching assistants (high school) work with me in the classroom. When you prepare your strategic plans, consider volunteers to be part of your instructional program. Establishing a good working relationship will produce many benefits.

> Freedom is not worth having if it does not include the freedom to make mistakes.
> —Mahatma Gandhi

Your "Bag of Tricks" Creates Success Stories:

Short and Long-Range Planning

Introduction

You have your road map, your teacher journey path, and your personal instructional style. Vision, mission, goals, objectives, organization, and decision-making are partners in strategic planning. Let us pick up your "bag of tricks," experience, wonder, and begin the process of short- and long-range planning.

Successful teaching requires all these types of plans: daily, weekly or monthly, short-range and long-range planning. The goals of these lesson plan formats make balanced progress and student involvement in the learning process a reality. It prevents disjointed and unrelated instruction and helps classroom experiences move along at a reasonable pace.

Remember, your goal is "to kiss as many frogs" as possible. Let us recall our educational road map and the stops we have made on the journey on behalf of all students. Your enthusiasm and positive attitude will open doors for students personally and academically. Yes, you are making a difference in students' lives because teaching is an act of heart, soul, mind, and body—your whole being. When you find the content and teaching draining, and there are many added responsibilities, and you have to be accountable to a variety of people and requirements, remember your original goal and interest that first attracted you to teaching in the first place. We can rekindle our interest in teaching by:

1. Taking time and read your areas of interest.
2. Attending workshops and in-services.
3. Keeping a daily journal of thoughts and discoveries.
4. Being around people who are positive and creative.
5. Talking with people who share your same interests.

We want to explore strategic planning and the kinds of lesson plans that will excite students and involve them in learning. Your "bag of tricks" and flexible lesson plans will reenergize classroom programs and connect students with you and create more success stories. Education is a complicated process, and lesson planning is one of the basic needs for organized learning inside and outside the classroom.

> He who deigns to teach must never cease to learn.
> —Aristotle

> The whole point of education is to turn mirrors into windows.
> —Sydney J. Harris

> The job of an educator is to teach students to see vitality in themselves.
> —Joseph Campbell

Lesson Planning

"Oh no! I'm not prepared with my lessons today." "You know, I'm not sure of my lesson goals and objectives this week." "I don't have materials for my experiment on Wednesday." I know these statements are not coming from you. Your plans are in place and prepared in advance. But, if you don't plan well, you will experience some potential problems.

For example:

1. Unclear goals and objectives make lessons confusing.
2. Students will never fully achieve objectives if there is confusion.
3. A demonstration lesson day and necessary materials or equipment is not available.
4. Assessment is difficult to identify because the objective is unclear.
5. Lesson skills and learning are reduced, and this frustrates teachers and students.

Be enthusiastic! Have a positive attitude! Organize! Make good decisions! Keep your vision, mission, goals, and objectives in front of you at all times. Teachers, plan! Plan! Plan! Then watch your students involved in learning multiply their accomplishments.

Comprehensive and consistent short- and long-range planning is similar to this saying: "A nail is a simple machine." Go ahead and "hit the nail on the head" with meaningful strategic planning and a major step toward successes for both teachers and students.

Step One: Pre-Planning Considerations

1. Curriculum: Guidelines, standards, benchmarks, grade level expectations, and prerequisite skills needed for competency
2. Learning: Check for individual student learning styles, prior knowledge of skills or subjects, strengths and weaknesses
3. Organization: Good decision-making, clear goals and objectives, authentic assessments, materials and equipment
4. Planning: Plan units and lessons for consistency of content and skill development

Step Two: Lesson Considerations

1. Time management.
2. Review of previous lesson or skill.
3. Overview of the lesson and activities.
4. Introduce concept or skills.
5. Practice, discussion, or activity.
6. Review and summarize.
7. Assessment (formal or informal).

Step Three: Post-Lesson Considerations

1. Evaluate successes and needs for improvement.
2. Review assessment for follow-up lessons.
3. Provide feedback and vary the format for multi-intelligences.

Let us pause on our journey and review some major stops on our educational road map. The classroom environment, teacher procedures, student interest, respect, and consistent discipline are enhanced by your effective and productive lesson plans.

Evaluation and self-evaluation are critical tools to refine teaching skills, assess objectives, and pinpoint weaknesses and strengths. Finally, all plans and lesson implementations should be clear to administrators, substitute teachers, parents, and especially students.

As we resume our educational journey, let us explore long-range, short-range, and general lesson plan steps, techniques, and formats.

Long-Range Planning

The long-range plan is an overview of units with developmental goals, standards, expected outcomes, important concepts, and themes for the various subjects. Long-range plans are flexible, regularly evaluated, and adjustments are made throughout the school year in some of these ways: creating additions, making deletions, using new projects, or selecting alternate lessons.

A collaborative approach to long-range planning ensures the incorporation of standards, skills, correct materials, appropriate concepts, and lessons that meet individual student and group needs (remedial and gifted). Evaluation, authentic assessment process, and informative feedback are essential to the overall format for the year. Finally, an individual teacher or a team approach by grade level or subject area teachers provides a solid academic foundation approach for the students, parents, school, and the district.

• • • • • • • • • • • • •

Long-Range Strategic Plan Sample
English Grammar and
Writing (grades sixth through ninth)

There are as many long-range strategic plans as there are teachers in the profession. The major lesson plan formats used by the majority of educators are effective, but teachers also adapt the categories to suit their individual needs, goals, students, skills, and subjects. This sample is one of many long-range styles for planning lessons.

Over the past twenty years, I have come to the realization and understanding of the best methods to organize long-range grammar and writing plans. Within the last five years, I have incorporated a variety of lesson plan models to offer students consistent grammar skill development, listening, speaking, observation, activities, and writing throughout the curriculum. My experience with student successes in these two subject areas are an intensive drill and application of these grammar and writing skills on a daily basis for a twenty-five to thirty-five minute time period. A critical element of this alternate planning is consistent evaluation of student growth and self-evaluation of lesson plan effectiveness.

Criteria for Instruction (standards and benchmarks are located in the curriculum drawer.)

1. Lesson plan objective per skill area
2. Teacher's edition suggestions: individual student, challenge assignments, etc.
3. Workbook practice and reteaching sentences
4. Board work
5. Question and answers
6. Dictation
7. Written: paragraphs, various kinds of creative writing, and essays
8. Unit and diagnostic tests
9. Teacher resource guide
10. Literature curriculum suggestions
11. Vocabulary curriculum suggestions
12. Supplementary materials

The Writing Process

1. Writing styles: descriptive, narrative, persuasive, opinion, instructional, and compare and contrast
2. Writing steps: prewriting, first draft, revising, proofing, and publish (final draft)

3.   Essay steps: introductory paragraph, main
     paragraphs, and concluding paragraph
Grammar and Writing Activities

1.   Class newspaper
2.   Creative writing for art and music
3.   Writing a children's book
4.   Writing journals
5.   Games and word puzzles
6.   Writing poetry
7.   Writing plays and skits

Student's understanding and learning of skills varies greatly on a daily basis. Individual and small group tutoring will be available to students when there is a need for reinforcement of specific skills and writing practice.

The grammar and writing curriculum, schedule, standards, and benchmarks will follow the same rationale and organization as the annual overview. Individual and small group drill, oral, and written assignments will be offered with above grade level sentences, paragraphs, skill development, grammar and its use in writing and related projects ideas.

Advanced Grammar Textbook and Materials

1.   Classroom textbook series for grades 7 and
     8
2.   *Hayes* and similar drill workbook for grades
     8–12

3. *Grammar and Composition* by Houghton Mifflin English (grades 9–12)
4. *Essentials of English* by Joseph Bellafiore for (grades 9–12)

Grammar and Writing Schedule

September
1. Sentence structure
2. Descriptive writing
3. Project: puzzles

October
1. Phrases, clauses, sentences
2. Prepositional phrases
3. Adverb, adjective, and noun clauses
4. Writing to express an opinion
5. Project: music and art

November–December
1. Compound and complex sentences
2. Sentence structure
3. Writing in complete sentences
4. Writing in narrative form
5. Project: class newspaper

January
1. Nouns: all kinds and how they are used correctly in sentences and paragraphs
2. Begin section on verbs
3. Writing instructions

4. Project: write original plays or skits

February
1. Verbs: all kinds and how to use them correctly in sentences and paragraphs
2. Writing to persuade
3. Project: writing a children's book

March
1. Adjectives and adverbs
2. Writing to compare and contrast
3. Project: writing poetry

April
1. Punctuation and capitalization
2. Writing a news article
3. Project: research work

May–June
1. Pronouns
2. Review of grammar topics and writing techniques and styles
3. Project: oral presentations
(Robert–Teacher)

Short-Term Planning

The short-term plan reveals the goals, outcomes, subjects, skills, and time allotment for a period of time (weekly or monthly). This format is helpful for groups of students in various subjects, projects, science experiments, and research assignments. There are various formats and lesson forms for short-term planning.

Creating Your Own Book Project
February Class Work and Homework

Learning Outcomes (Grades 5–10)

1. To reinforce organizational and time management skills.
2. To help students review, learn, describe, and apply the writing process steps.
3. To remind students to identify and use the five senses in their writing.
4. To offer practice for writing details, tone, and establishing characters, settings, and climax in their books.
5. To offer students the opportunity to reinforce writing a good beginning and ending.
6. To provide students with a step-by-step approach to handling grammar, punctuation, and proofreading skills.

General Directions

1. Your story and book must be typed (use 12 or 14 font).
2. Your final published story and book may be vertically or horizontally bound.
3. Your story and book may be printed with large letters, but in black ink only.

4. Your final copy of your book should be typed or printed on quality paper.
5. Your story must be written for a specific grade level: K, 1, 2, 3, or 4.
6. You must include the following:
   a. Title page: title of your story, your name as author, name of your illustrator, and a colored drawing or symbol that represents your story.
   b. Dedication page
   c. Introduction
7. Your book must have colored drawings or symbols that relate to your story.
8. Your book must have a hardback cover.
9. Additional directions will be given in class.

Helpful Story Writing Tips

1. Start thinking:
   a. Audience - Do you know who you are writing for when you start your story?
   b. Purpose - Do you want to amuse, bring mystery, adventure, or teach a lesson?
   c. Share - Remember, you will be publishing your story in the form of a book.
2. Choose your story ideas:
   a. Brainstorm and list story ideas.
   b. Include specific details.
   c. Will I enjoy writing about my topic?
   d. Will others enjoy reading it?
3. What makes a great story?

a. Characters - Create interesting, believable characters.
b. Setting - Establish a setting by giving details (where and when).
c. Plot - Develop a plot that includes a conflict, resolution, and a climax. Give hints about what will happen later in the story.
d. Story events - Events must make sense and have a clear beginning, middle, and end.
e. Dialogue - Details bring characters, setting, and events to life.
f. Viewpoint - Tell your story from a single point of view.
g. Create - Write your story with mood or emotion.
h. Beginning - Write a beginning that introduces characters and settings.
i. Ending. - Resolve story conflicts and answer questions your readers might have.

Timeline for Completion of your Book

January 30-February 9
Final proposal, first draft of story, and preliminary drawings

February 10
Final Due Date: Friday, February 10
February 13–15
First draft of title page, dedication, and introduction

February 16
Final Due Date: Thursday, February 16

February 21
Challenge: Due Date: (complete book and story) 3 grades + 40 points + 3 study credits

February 28
Final Due Date for completion of book and story by everyone

Proposal

Name: _____ Date: _____

1. I will be creating one book. _____
2. I will be creating two or more books _____
   for a challenge grade.
3. Illustrator's name:_____ ____myself
4. Introduction–name: _____ ____myself
5. Dedication person: _____
6. I am writing my story and publishing my
   book for the following grade level:
   _____ Grade 1   _____Grade 2
   _____ Grade 1   _____Other_____
7. Type of story you are writing:
   _____ adventure   _____ mystery
   _____ nonfiction   _____ comedy
   _____ humor   _____ fantasy
   _____ science fiction
   _____ other:
8. Other information: _____

   _____

9. _____
   Student signature   Date
10. _____
    Approval   Date

Student Debate Steps

A debate involves taking sides on an issue and then presenting your arguments for or against that issue. A statement of that issue is called a "proposition." The people who support the proposition are called the "Affirmative Team." They agree with the statement. Those who disagree with it are called the "Negative Team." While formal debates follow a strict format, informal debates have various structures. The format below is an example of an informal debate. Each statement is usually given by a different team member.

Opening statement by Affirmative Team 3 minutes
Opening statement by Negative Team   3 minutes
(Three minutes are allowed for teams to prepare rebuttals.)

Rebuttal by Affirmative Team   2 minutes
Rebuttal by Negative Team   2 minutes
Second Affirmative statement   3 minutes
Second Negative statement   3 minutes
(Three minutes are allowed for teams to prepare rebuttals and closing statements.)

Rebuttal and Closing by Affirmative Team 2 minutes
Rebuttal and Closing by Negative Team 2 minutes

Note:

An "opening statement" introduces a team's position and offers important evidence.

A "rebuttal" is a team's response to its opponent's arguments.

A "second statement" is a team's chance to expand upon their ideas and evidence.

• • • • • • • • • • • • • •

Suggested Persuasive Essay Topics

1. There should be greater control by the government over music.
2. There should be laws against flag burning.
3. Public schools should allow for a moment of silence and/or prayer.
4. Religious leaders should be allowed to speak at graduations.
5. The death penalty should be abolished.
6. Police officers should have greater freedom in car searches.
7. Young people who commit crimes should be treated like adults.
8. Public schools should be able to require all students to wear uniforms.
9. There should be equal funding for men's and women's sports in schools.
10. Should you be permitted to purchase or buy whatever you want to with your own money?
11. Should you be permitted to get any style of haircut you want?

12. Should you be allowed to go anywhere you want to with your friends?
13. Should you be required to do chores around the house? Which jobs?
14. Should you be allowed to take lessons to play any musical instrument you like?
15. Should you have homework assignments every night?
16. Does society have a right to put someone to death?
17. Should you be able to have the freedom to choose your own bedtime?
18. Should you be able to watch any television program?
19. Should kids between the ages of ten and thirteen be dropped off at the mall without adult supervision?
20. Should animals be used for scientific experimentation?
21. Television is better than books.
22. Girls have it better than boys.
23. Cats make better pets than dogs.
24. Animals should not be kept in cages.
25. Computers should replace teachers.

Daily Lesson Planning

The daily lesson plan is a written account of what the teacher hopes to happen and how effective the value of the goals, outcomes, and classroom experiences offer student involvement and learning for that specific day. There are many lesson plan styles and formats that focus on particular aspects of the instructional process. The following are considerations for most lesson plan formats.

Step One: Topic

Lesson title, subject area, and grade level are part of the topic.

Step Two: Goals

Goals are written in general terms and provide expectations for what students will be able to do by the end of the lesson or unit.

Step Three: Objectives

Objectives are knowledge and skills obtained during the lesson or unit, and this includes performance observed from assessment.

Step Four: Materials

Materials, equipment, and use of time are needed for the lesson or unit development.

Step Five: Prerequisites

What knowledge, skills, and concepts are already acquired in advance of your objectives.

What must students know and be able to do before the lesson.

Step Six: Lesson Plan Procedures

Introduction: The introduction of a lesson provides students with these key elements:

1. Interest and motivation for the topic.
2. Introduction to the main lesson points.
3. Presentation of the lesson, perhaps using some of these methods:

a. ask questions
b. tell a story
c. show a video
d. prepare a demonstration
e. show illustrations
f. check students' previous understanding , experience, and knowledge

Presentation: Students will be enthusiastic for your lesson if you implement these steps:

1. Use short sentences to explain directions and skills.
2. Provide adequate time allotments for activities.
3. Use basic vocabulary.
4. Speak clearly.
5. Pause at critical times during your explanations.
6. Use pictures, videos, objects, gestures, etc.
7. Check the flow and progress of your lesson.

Closure or Conclusion: Review ideas and provide feedback.

1. Review skills and concepts and offer feedback.
2. Feedback is helpful in these ways: corrects a student's missing skills, reinforces learning, provides directions for projects, and creates reasonable homework assignments.
3. Plan activities that suggest enrichment or remediation assignments as a follow-up to the lesson.

Remember, you don't always have to stick to a well-made plan. Flexibility is important, and have your "bag of tricks" ready for emergencies. Each teacher uses a general plan outline but has their own individual style, situation, goals and objectives, and school requirements. Be alert to what students are learning: new skills, formula, or concept.

Step Seven: Assessment and Evaluation

The evaluation of objectives is crucial for focusing on students' ability to understand the lesson after practice and application. Practice involves repetition, experiment, and discovery in a controlled classroom environment. Application takes what students have practiced and applies it to real-life situations.

Step Eight: Self-Evaluation

Each day of a teacher is busy, rushed, and there are a variety of duties that need to be performed. You may be tempted to skip this step, but don't you dare! Self-evaluation is a powerful tool that will help you evaluate your teaching, lessons, and refine your instructional style. Take a few moments each day to write brief notes on your lesson plans, and you will discover surprises of successes and other ways of improving your presentation.

Alternate or Contingency Planning

Alternate or contingency plans are a good idea in case lessons don't go as you planned. These are some actual situations for using alternate plans:

1. Practice exercises are too easy for students, but you want to check their ability; you ask the class to do the even-numbered items.
2. Students arrive in the morning and state the homework was too difficult. You ask questions, have them complete the work in class, and assign a similar homework assignment to strengthen skill development of the lesson.
3. You are going to show a video as part of your lesson. The VCR makes funny noises and has eaten the tape. You select one of your alternate plans and divide the class into groups of four. You proceed to give clear directions, time frame, allow discussion, and reporting back to the class (allow two days).

You are in the faculty room talking to your colleagues. A teacher asks what is so important about lesson planning. Can anything bad happen? Absolutely! A teacher can wander, get off the track, and fail to accomplish the objectives. I could go on! Although, there are days even strong and consistent lesson plans do not flow smoothly, and there are other situations which may make lesson implementation difficult. Your long-range plans, alternate plans, and your "bag of tricks" will make you as a teacher more confident, lessons move successfully, and assessments more productive.

The "bottom line" that students are involved in learning, assessment, feedback, and evaluation will help check progress and understanding.

Teachers today are restricted to teach by state standards, district benchmarks, scope and sequence, content, grade level skills, and various curriculum requirements. My own experiences and interviews with teacher friends, other educators, administrators, and schools led me to discover many similarities. The following are some major examples of lesson plan styles.

Lesson Plan Style One
Grades K-1 (Unit: three days or one week)

1. Topic (Title)
2. Goals
3. Objectives
4. Materials (Rationale)
5. Content (Prerequisites)
6. Instructional procedures (Lesson plan procedures)
7. Assessment and evaluation (Evaluation procedures)
8. Self-evaluation (Assessment)

Topic:
   Eleanor Roosevelt:
   A Leader Who Helps People

Goals:
1. To read a biography about Eleanor Roosevelt.
2. To learn six historical facts.
3. To develop a stronger sense of her humanitarian work.

4. To introduce the word *humanitarian*.
5. To encourage students to help others.

Objectives:
1. To introduce students to Eleanor Roosevelt, the person.
2. To show how she cared for people.
3. To discuss the concept of leadership.

Materials:
1. Biography of Eleanor Roosevelt
2. Art paper
3. Crayons
4. Writing paper
5. Pencils

Content:
1. Read children's biographies of Eleanor Roosevelt.
2. Use questions, answers, and storytelling techniques to talk about her life and activities.
3. Show pictures of Eleanor Roosevelt engaged in various humanitarian activities.
4. Post pictures on the bulletin board weekly.
5. Have children draw pictures of Eleanor Roosevelt and her activities.

Instructional Procedures:
1. Present questions for discussion on leadership.
2. Read a biography of Eleanor Roosevelt.

3. Ask questions on the reading.
4. Answer and write: What can you do to become a humanitarian?

Assessment and Evaluation:
1. Write a poem about Eleanor Roosevelt as a leader.
2. Make a drawing about her leadership.
3. Write a letter telling your family what we learned about Eleanor Roosevelt as a leader.

Teacher Self-Evaluation
(Teacher: Carmela, teacher and friend)

Lesson Plan Style One
Grades 7–8 (Unit: one or two weeks)

1. Topic (Title)
2. Goals
3. Objectives
4. Materials (Rationale)
5. Content (Prerequisites)
6. Instructional procedures (Lesson plan procedures)
7. Assessment and evaluation (Evaluation procedures)
8. Self-evaluation (Assessment and evaluation)

Topic:
　　Literature: "Song of the Trees"
　　By Mildred D. Taylor; pages 110–124

Goals:

1. To reinforce setting and conflict in a story.
2. To present the qualities of a historical setting.
3. To use techniques to extend a story.
4. To discuss the theme, "Doing what is right."

Objectives:

1. To understand setting and how it affects the characters and the conflict in a story.
2. To discuss and review how the Great Depression affects the conflicts of this story.
3. To write an extension of the story describing what will happen to the characters over time.
4. To discuss in groups and write individually about choices.

Materials:

1. Writing paper
2. Pens
3. Pencils
4. Drawing paper
5. Markers or crayons
6. Review assignment.

Content:
1. General class discussion:
   a. What is the setting of the story?
   b. What is the Great Depression of 1930?
2. What are some situations in which you had to make a difficult choice?
   a. Student discussion groups
   b. Each group reports back to the class
3. Story vocabulary: write word correctly in sentences, and use the word correctly in a one-page story.

Instructional Procedures:
1. Read the story and use the thinking map to discover the different ways to express conflict in a story.
2. Answer questions in your notebooks.
3. Individual and small group work:
   a. Compose a timeline and organize the details within the story.
   b. Create evaluation questions by using your timelines.
4. Challenge assignment: complete a "mini" research on "Different Kinds of Trees" using three resources.

Assessment and Evaluation:
1. Imagine that you are the author of this story. Extend the story by writing what will happen over the next two years to the Logans.
   a. What will happen to the trees?

b. Include dialogue in your story.
2. Setting and conflict questions:
    a. What are the differences and similarities about the trees?
    b. How long has the Logan family been affected by the Great Depression?

Teacher Self-Evaluation

Lesson Plan Style One
    Grades 9–12 (two to four weeks)
1. Topic (Title)
2. Goals
3. Objectives
4. Materials (Rationale)
5. Content (Prerequisites)
6. Instructional procedures (Lesson plan procedures)
7. Assessment and evaluation (Evaluation procedures)
8. Self-evaluation

Topic:
    Technical Theater High School
    Set Design
Goals:

1. To learn how to analyze a script.
2. To learn how to adapt a rough floor plan.
3. To learn how to adapt a scale.
4. To be able to define terms.

Objectives:

1. To practice and design a rough sketch of a floor plan.
2. To adapt a floor plan to a scale floor plan.
3. To create and draw a three-dimensional model of a set design.

Materials:
  (not listed)
  Content:

1. Introduce the unit: evaluation, define terms, show a stage, flat, and set.
2. Explain the uses and advantages of stage scenery.
3. Review with students the plays they have chosen.
4. Look and comment on student rough floor plans.
5. Demonstrate how to use compass, t-square, templates, wood, cardboard, etc.
6. Reexamine final rough drawings for approval.

Instructional Procedures:
1. Work on student floor plans and answer questions.
2. Review stage terms and prepare students for a test.
3. Continue work on floor plan models.

4. Take test on set design and vocabulary terms.
5. Discuss the final steps in the model building process.

Assessment and Evaluation:

1. Work for next three days on models and scripts.
2. Work for the next four days with each student on their production project for an oral presentation.
3. Oral presentations.
4. Major grade for this unit:

   a. Project
   b. Oral presentation
   c. Neatness and use of tools
   d. Stay within the scale drawings

Teacher Self-Evaluation (Teacher: Allen Moore)

Outcome Lesson Plan Style Two
Grades 5–6 (First Week)

1. Outcomes
2. Preparation
3. Procedures and activities
4. Closure and assessment
5. Materials

Outcomes (important)

1. To identify ways in which agriculture changed human life.
2. To understand how surpluses led to specialization and trade.
3. To explain how trade fosters an exchange of goods and ideas.

Preparation (outcomes)

1. Read, discuss, and take notes on Lesson One.
2. Identify causes and effects on a chart of the development of agriculture and how it led to civilization.
3. Explain and discuss the importance of vocabulary words related to the lesson.

Procedures and Activities (outcomes)

1. Individual project: You are a traveler to Catal Huyuk. What can you learn from visiting the city? (Directions given along with an information sheet).

   a. Agriculture
   b. Homes and where to stay as a traveler
   c. How to purchase food and supplies

2. Art project: draw and create two home styles in Catal Huyuk and write several paragraphs describing your drawing.
3. Answer questions on page 83.

Closure and Assessment (outcomes)

1. Small group work and reporting back to the class.
   a. What is involved in domesticating plants and animals?
   b. How did trade help the city to grow?
   c. How did agriculture change the way people interacted with their environment?

2. Written assignment: Select an occupation you would like to have during the New Stone Age. Write two or three paragraphs in which you tell what made it possible for them to do your job and what your work adds to the community.
3. Review and preparation for Lesson One test.

Self-Evaluation (Teacher–Marsha Allen)

Outcome Lesson Plan Style Two
Grades 7–8 (three days to one week)

1. Outcomes
2. Preparation

3. Procedures and activities
4. Closure and assessment
5. Materials

Outcomes (important)

1. To review, identify, and apply the various forms of nouns orally and in writing.
2. To discuss, distinguish, and use singular and plural nouns correctly in sentences.
3. To learn, identify, and use possessive nouns correctly in sentences and paragraphs.

Preparation (outcomes)

1. Oral practice and examples
2. Written practice:
    a. Dictation
    b. Extra practice
    c. Writing experience

Procedures (outcomes)

1. Workbook exercises
2. More practice from supplementary materials (textbook)

Self-evaluation (Teacher-Robert Grossi)

Madeline Hunter's Lesson Plan Style Three
Primary-Elementary Grades (first week)

1. Objectives
2. Purpose
3. Anticipatory set
4. Input
5. Modeling
6. Check for understanding
7. Guided practice
8. Independent practice

"Madeline Hunter devoted much of her career to an analysis of what makes instruction effective. She identifies instructional principles in the areas of motivation, reinforcement transfer rate, and degree of learning and retention. Dr. Hunter's research showed that effective teachers have a methodology when planning and presenting a lesson."

James McNair, a writer and educator, offers an example of this variation on Madelyn Hunter's lesson plan design. Please take note that Dr. Hunter's lesson plan format is very comprehensive and complete. I am presenting this popular style of planning as an example for you, but in a summarized form.

Objectives

1. To demonstrate a working knowledge of words and definitions from the story.
2. To include words from the story, *Alexander and the Wind-up Mouse,* by Leo Lionni.
3. To answer story questions from several categories based on Bloom's cognitive domain.

Standards:

1. Predict what a passage is about based on titles and illustrations.
2. Identify words and construct meanings from text, illustrations, and charts.
3. Increase comprehension rereading and discussion.

Materials: book, projector, copies of illustrations, word puzzle, board, chalk, art supplies

Anticipatory Set

1. Teacher asks questions about a mouse.
2. Teacher shows a copy of the book and gives a brief introduction to the story.
3. Teacher informs the class that a projector will be used to tell the story so students can see the illustrations.

Input

1. Read the story slowly.
2. Provide a discussion about living things.
3. Encourage students to think of story events and their own lives.
4. Review words from the word list.
5. Write the words in a spelling journal with definitions.

Modeling

1. Construct a word puzzle to complete in class.

2. Engage in a drawing activity where students recreate their favorite part of the story.

Check for Understanding

1. Memory skills–recall events.
2. Translation–express key concepts.
3. Interpretation–identify values and characters.
4. Extrapolation–predict alternate outcomes.
5. Application–identify available solutions.
6. Analysis–understand the relationships between the characters.
7. Synthesis–form a hypothesis from the story and re-create different characters and settings.
8. Evaluation–decide if the characters were doing the right thing.

Guided Practice

1. Storytelling for imagery
2. Discussion and questions
3. Word recognition
4. Word definitions for understanding
5. Word puzzles to reinforce comprehension
6. Update spelling journals

Independent Practice
Students will engage in an artistic activity by selecting their favorite scene and recreating on art paper. The teacher will offer complete directions. Students

are to write sentences or a paragraph describing their drawing.

Closure (teacher)

1. Demonstrate a working understanding of story words and how they are used today.
2. Introduce language arts and science concepts to assist students in knowing fiction and facts.

Other Lesson Plan Styles
Focus Lesson Plan

1. Uses some of the categories in General Lesson Plan One
2. Focus activity
3. Teaching procedures (methods)
4. Progress check (throughout the lesson)
5. Student participation
6. Closure
7. Check for student needs
8. Management techniques

Launching Lesson
    The beginning of a unit or chapter should arouse interest and give an overview for students.

1. To arouse interest in the study of…
2. To stimulate questions about…
3. To make students aware of…

4. To present a preview of…

Development Lesson

New material is presented; ask questions and share information.

Objectives:

1. To present…
2. To find out the effects of…
3. To become acquainted with…

Directed Study Lesson

Students read, find information, or answer questions. They are encouraged to raise additional questions and draw conclusions.

Objectives:

1. To gain more information about…
2. To increase knowledge of…
3. To further develop the understanding of…

Independent Study Lesson

Students are given an opportunity to complete research from basic textbooks and supplementary materials.

Objectives:

1. To learn more about…

2. To use reference books and supplementary texts...

Discussion Lesson

An independent study lesson at home or school following discussion groups or teacher/student discussion time.

Objectives: knowledge of, better understand, acquire, and work effectively in groups

Sample Lesson Planning Evaluation Form

Teachers, this form uses the following criteria to check goals and objectives, lesson plan sections, activities, successes, and needs for improvement. I want you to be aware of how effective my plans were organized, adapted, and provided active learning for students of various ability levels. You may adapt this form and key to suit your own needs.

Teacher name: _____

Date: _____

Key: S = Successful A = Acceptable
        NI = Needs Improvement

_____1. Were goals and objectives clear and measurable?

_____2. Did my lesson plan format provide consistent skills and steps?

____	Outcomes	____	Activities
____	Introduction	____	Assessment
____	Procedures	____	Feedback

_____3. Was there a balance of activities as to the lesson theme and maturity of students and their ability levels?

_____4. Was provision made for each student to have time to complete the work?
(time management)

_____5. Was there a balance between large and small group and individual work and activities?

_____6. Were new materials and activities paced to the students' needs and interest?

_____7. Were there enough familiar routines and learning activities to give students security?

_____8. Did students use their time wisely to explore, complete activities, or experiment?

_____9. Was special consideration given to planning for special projects, special needs, and advanced students?

_____10. Was the planning for this lesson part of the overall strategic plans?

_____11. Was assessment, self-evaluation, and feedback included as part of the overall lesson plan?

Comments:

_____
_____
_____

Assessment Tools: Performance and Authentic Assessments

Introduction

An assessment of a person becomes more authentic when there is communication, understanding, respect, and knowledge shared in a positive and friendly manner. Teachers, be positive about translating your planning considerations as a goal to improve teaching and increase student learning. The assessment of your students academically and their growth personally will be a reality for you and your students. If you are laying the groundwork for your strategic planning, it is important to include authentic and performance assessment opportunities.

Authentic Assessment

What makes something authentic? It is the representation of real work, performance of samples, tasks, outcomes that are used beyond school, and applied knowledge and skills to life. The most important reason to develop and implement authentic assessment is to improve teaching and increase learning.

In Authentic Performance Assessment, students not only perform or demonstrate specific behaviors that are to be assessed, but also do so in a real-life context.

—Carol Meyer, Evaluation Specialist; Beaverton School District, Oregon

Authentic Curriculum

(significant, important to life, outcomes)

Student as Worker

Authentic Instruction Authentic Assessment (instructional strategies, practices, direct examination of performance and activities that produce learning by means of worthwhile tasks)

Marilyn Tabor, Workshop for Teachers, "Curriculum and Assessment,"
Irvine Unified School District.

Assessments offer students opportunities to strengthen academic performance, personal growth, and develop responsibility in the following ways:

1. Encourages students to be active in self-evaluation.
2. Creates a variety of monitoring methods for authentic assessment.
3. Helps students to build self-confidence at all ability levels.
4. Describes assessment designs that teachers, students, and parents are able to understand lesson goals and objectives clearly.
5. Translate assessment results into instructional plans by teachers.
6. Students' capacity to use self-assessment will help to improve learning.

7. Monitor student understanding and impact on teaching and learning.

Kate Jamentz, "Making Sure That Assessment Improves Performance,"
Educational Leadership, 3/94.

Performance Assessment

Performance assessment refers to responses that examine knowledge, skills, and concepts. Students may answer questions, create a product, design a graph or chart, make an oral presentation, or provide a demonstration. Authentic assessment refers to the manner in which students respond and answer in real-life situations. Teachers must set up this assessment carefully for authentic results by using these considerations: standards, criteria, conditions, main points, and requirements.

I have been fortunate throughout my teaching career to attend a variety of workshops, seminars, and collaborate with many friends and outstanding educators. My instructional plans have included performance assessment, but authentic assessment tools have brought me closer to the "heart and soul" of teaching and a greater connection with students and their successes as individuals and students. Thank you, everyone, for my progress, and these are some of my experiences and observations about assessment.

Authentic Performance Assessment

1. Organizes before lesson and learning.
2. Concentrates on successes in student work.
3. Offers students a variety of tasks.
4. Requires students to think and problem solve with real-life situations.
5. Provides scenarios and challenges from real life.
6. Continues learning to the next step.

Testing Practices (Performance)

1. Organizes after the lesson and learning.
2. Evaluates specific assignments.
3. Is usually limited to one-answer questions.
4. Recognizes or identifies the right answer.
5. Completes drills on a variety of elements.
6. The learning cycle ends after the lesson.

There are many challenges teachers face each day, as well as rewards seeing students grow personally and academically. The importance of self-evaluation and assessment are productive tools for reflection, and this letter from a former student depicts the collaboration necessary between the teacher and student for those skills.

> Dear Mr. Grossi,
> Thank you for the sensitivity you had shown me for my needs and hurts. Your willingness to reach out to me, even in my silence, helped me believe

in myself. The writing, grammar, and research lessons and assignments have helped me to become a better writer by outlining, completing a "rough draft," knowing how to proofread and revise. Time management helps to organize my school, social, and sports life. But the basic skills you taught me and others about evaluating our work and progress has moved us to the next level of knowledge.

You told me, "It may not be easy at times, but in those hard times you will find a stronger sense of yourself." I will remember these and other words and move on and hope for the future.

Love and Thanks,
—Maggie Di Angelo (tenth grade student)

Reflections: Maggie, thank you for being open to discover the talents within you. Your dedication to learning reminds me again of how positive approaches affect a student's progress. The continuing review and self-evaluation of my lesson plans are important, as you have shown by your acceptance of my showing you different approaches to learning.

General Assessment

Classroom assessment and evaluation techniques promote useful feedback on what, how much, and how well students are learning. Teachers can use this information to refocus or expand their teaching to enhance the quality of effective learning for everyone. Regular practice of assessment and self-evaluation skills will empower both teachers and students to improve the quality of learning in the classroom.

Assessment and evaluation tools are ongoing and partners in the teaching-learning cycle. It is critical that these procedures correspond with goals, curriculum objectives, instructional practices, and the developmental characteristics of your students. Remember, it's important for all teachers to communicate with students all assessment and evaluation plans and results to help them become more self-directed learners.

1. *Assessment* is gathering information on regular or daily basis in order to understand the student's abilities, learning style, and needs. The data affords the teacher a chance to adapt teaching strategies for quality classroom assessment of instruction and planning.
2. *Evaluation* is gathered at the completion of a unit, end of an activity, or reporting period along with daily assessments which provide information on student progress.

These are some areas for assessment and evaluation processes we should consider when we are involved in our long-range planning. These suggestions are either for elementary, middle school, or high school or could be adapted for your students and grade level.

1. Teacher-directed lessons and assessments
2. Teacher observations of cooperative groups

3. Authentic tasks related to real-life situations
4. Responses to teacher-created tests
5. Teacher-written observation
6. Portfolio collections
7. Daily work samples
8. Self-evaluation assignments
9. Evaluation checklists
10. Assessment questions
11. Bulletin board displays
12. Posters
13. Photo essay
14. Group work
15. Multimedia presentations
16. Designing a web page
17. Open-ended questions
18. Videotape a task performance
19. Journals
20. Oral interviews
21. Story retelling
22. Writing samples
23. Projects
24. Reports
25. Discussions
26. Graphs and graphic organizers
27. Drama: role-playing and skits
28. Writing: to inform, descriptive, expository, persuasive, opinion, compare and contrast

Students gain an understanding of the skill, lesson, and progress they have made by self-reflection and evaluation. It is essential they recognize the processes and learning strategies so improvement is shown in real-life situations and facts. Guidance and direction in self-evaluation offers students confidence and responsibility. Teachers need to provide consistent training and encouragement for students to discover results of self-reflection and help them take charge of learning.

These questions provide students with assessment examples to reflect on their responses to their understanding and the completion of an assignment.

• • • • • • • • • • • • •

Primary (K-2)

1. What kind of work is this?
2. Why is this work important to you?
3. How did you try your best?

Intermediate (3–5)

1. What makes this your best work?
2. What problems did you encounter?
3. What ways have you improved as a _____?
4. What did you do when you were "stuck"?

Middle and High School (7–12)

1. What are your special strengths in this work?
2. How does this work show that you are good as a _____?
3. How is this like or different from your earlier work?

4. How are you accomplishing your goal(s)?
5. What did you learn about _____ ___ from this work?
6. How are you changing as a writer?
7. What are some challenges you are facing in this work?
8. How would you describe your thinking?
9. What do you need to do next time in order to be a better _____?

Portfolio Assessment

There are numerous assessment and evaluation techniques which are effective and provide teachers with feedback on lessons, student learning, and review of daily, short, and long-term plans. I would like to describe some benefits of having student folders with completed assignments for teachers and parents to review progress and learning. I would like to share some options for student work folders but emphasize the portfolio process. What are you able to place in a student's folder?

1. Observation notes and checklists
2. Conference summaries
3. Test results
4. Progress notes
5. Interview with students
6. Descriptions of student's abilities in learning and self-evaluation

7. Subject area assignments (possible ten to twelve samples)

I have used the student work collections and the portfolio process during my years in education.

Both student collection styles take time and effort on the part of the teacher, and teachers must be trained in each process. Students should be trained to self-evaluate and know the steps to check progress every two or three weeks. The rewards are tremendous. I was able to (1) check progress of each student on a regular basis, (2) train students on how to self-evaluate and check their own progress, (3) review lesson plans and make additions and strengthen skill areas, (4) provide regular feedback for student understanding.

Portfolios are work collections in which teachers help students develop criteria and teach them how to reflect and evaluate pieces of their work. Students would select their own work and attach evaluation questions or reasons for selecting a piece of work and progress made with that specific assignment. Teachers can also require certain types of work so a student's portfolio will be represented by a comprehensive work selection. This can be a challenge, but well worth the time. It was my goal in this process to set up portfolio days (or a week) on a monthly or quarterly basis. When you meet with small groups on these days, there is a sharing and discussion of selections, evaluation, and progress. It is important that you emphasize to students the importance self-analysis, self-evaluation, and goal-setting as part of their explanation.

Testing and Assessment

Assessment and evaluation are one of the main features of education. But teachers, administrators, districts, and parents measure a student's strengths and weaknesses by test scores to judge the quality of education. Testing forms and scores are important basic formats for assessment and commitment to high academic standards and school accountability. Unfortunately, teachers begin teaching to the test to raise scores at the expense of other meaningful learning activities and assessment tools. Testing or standardized testing can often provide a narrow view for teachers to offer students concrete information to improve learning for students at all level of abilities. It is essential to use testing as well as other forms of assessment and evaluation in your instructional plans.

The reality of the world today requires students to learn and know many facts and skills. The demands of the twenty-first century ask students to learn many concepts, higher-order thinking skills, comparison, analysis, inference, and evaluation. In addition, teamwork, communication, collaboration, and moral character are traits necessary to be successful as an adult and deal with real-life situations. Typical standardized tests aren't measuring these traits.

Many schools and districts are incorporating authentic and performance-based assessment questions and real-world examples into their standardized tests. This procedure provides more realistic results and feedback for teachers to review student learning and teaching methods.

Written Evaluation Form

Name: _____

Date: _____ Score: _____

Title of the Assignment:_____

_____

Organization and Preparation:

_____ 1. Were all directions followed carefully for this assignment?

_____ 2. Was the assignment turned in on the date due?

_____ 3. Did the assignment show organization, neatness, and careful preparation?

_____ 4. Did the student demonstrate positive effort and learning?

_____ 5. Was there enough specific information to cover the topic or answer the questions?

_____ 6. Did the student have a good understanding of the topic or assignment?

_____ 7. Did the assignment show a complete picture of the student's ability?

_____ 8. Did the student provide extra facts and information beyond the regular directions?

_____ 9. Did these areas show good proofreading and use of language: grammar
usage spelling, use of vocabulary, clarity of sentence, and paragraph structure?

_____ 10. Has the student demonstrated his or her overall potential in the preparation of this assignment?

Structure and Grammar Mechanics:

_____ 11. Are good writing techniques used effectively in this assignment?

_____ 12. Does the assignment reflect the student's strong effort, ability, and best use of time?

_____ 13. Does the overall sentence structure of this assignment make sense?

_____ 14. Does the overall paragraph structure make sense, flow smoothly, and relate to the topic?

_____ 15. Are the parts of speech used correctly and clearly throughout this assignment?

_____ 16. Does the student show correct usage of spelling and vocabulary?

_____ 17. Is punctuation used correctly and clearly in this assignment?

_____ 18. Does the student have a clear idea of writing techniques?

_____ 19. Does the student have a clear idea of good grammar and English skills?

_____ 20. Has the overall assignment demonstrated that the student proofread for clarity in grammatical structure, English skills, spelling, and writing techniques?

_____ Total

Key:

    5 = Working above and beyond grade level
    4 = Working above grade level
    3 = Working at grade level
    2 = Working below grade level
    1 = Needs improvement
    0 = Unable to evaluate

_____ Total

Score:
100–93 = A
92–90 = B +
89–86 = B
85–83 = B–
82–80 = C +
79–75 = C
74–70 = C–
69–65 = D
64–0 = F

Summary: Part One

Chapter One:

This chapter challenges your thinking and attitudes to know your values and beliefs as a classroom teacher and a school. This is a "we proposition" by all members of a school, regardless of the individuality of your teaching style and long-range planning. Yes, I am referring to the "heart and soul" of teaching and the positive connections you will make with your students. Take the time to reflect on these pre-planning considerations to inspire and energize your outcomes and create a realized picture of your educational targets.

1. Vision is an image and description of your classroom instructional plan.
2. The mission statement asks the questions, "Where will we be in five years?" and relates to the school's values and the vision.
3. Goals: Goals are broad statements and are measurable.
4. Objectives are specific and measurable statements of how goals are achieved in a year.
5. Philosophy is ideas and beliefs by teachers, the school, and the district.
6. Outcomes are changes in attitude, knowledge, behavior, and skills with students.

Let us continue to validate and recognize student and teacher progress by using the goal-setting process as a habit of success and a tool for continued improvement.

Chapter Two:

Good Thinking + Good Planning = Good Teaching!

As you enter into the process of thinking, organizing, and instructional planning, consider the growth of each person as a student and individual with gifts to develop and share with others. The real-life challenges and situations are the environments for these discoveries. I am aware of the outstanding instructors in many classrooms who "have a handle" on these suggestions, but let me just list them as reminders.
Students:

1. Should *listen* first, often, and with understanding.
2. Need an environment that helps them discover the *truth* about themselves without put-downs or negative talk.
3. Be able to *evaluate* their needs and progress.

Teachers:

1. Are models and "cheerleaders" for creating *trust* among all students.
2. Encourage *truth* as a core quality in the classroom.
3. *Know* students individually and academically.

4. Make vision, mission, goals, and objectives *real* and *alive*.
5. *Connect* with students and teachers and "speak from the heart."

Decisions! Decisions! Yes, the characteristics of a good teacher are decision-making and organization of learning. Teachers work with a variety of people and want students and fellow teachers to take responsibility, achieve successful results, and effectively be successful together for a common purpose.

Chapter Three:

Productive and successful teaching requires both daily, weekly, short-term, and long-term planning. There is no one best form for a daily lesson plan. The true test and value to any lesson plan is the effectiveness of learning for the student. Teachers and educators utilize various formats and categories of plan styles to suit their individual methods, needs, and students' academic and personal requirements. Let us review some examples of lesson plan types and styles in this chapter.

Lesson Plan Types:

Long-term plan:

A long-term plan is a brief overview or outline of goals, objectives, outcomes, skills, attitudes, materials, and units for the year.

Short-term plan:

A short-term plan is a modified long-range plan that includes goals, objectives, outcomes, skills, materials, lessons, and units for a week or month.

Daily lesson plans:

A daily lesson plan is a written account of what the teacher hopes to have happen during the teaching-learning activity and day.

General Lesson Plan Styles:

1. Topic
2. Goals
3. Objectives
4. Materials
5. Prerequisites
6. Lesson plan procedures
7. Assessment and evaluation
8. Self-evaluation

Other Lesson Plan Styles:

1. Outcome Lesson Plan Style
2. Madelyn Hunter Lesson Plan Style
3. Launching lesson begins a unit or chapter.
4. Development lesson reviews a specific section of a chapter.
5. Directed study lesson answers questions or searches for conclusions.

6. Independent study lesson researches various topics.
7. Discussion lessons

What do instructors think is a good lesson?

1. Use instructional goals and objectives.
2. Communicate outcomes in a clear manner.
3. Plan, pace, and organize.
4. Motivate students with a variety of teaching and learning strategies.
5. Use technology as a tool for research.
6. Check for student understanding.
7. Evaluate student performance.
8. Provide for feedback from students.
9. Provide a summary of the lesson or skill.

What do students think is a good lesson?

1. What is the teacher trying to accomplish in the lesson?
2. Is the subject and lesson well-paced, interesting, motivating, and challenging?
3. Does the content relate to previously learned concepts?
4. Does the teacher not assign excessive or useless work?

Chapter Four:

Assessment is one of the main components of education. Teachers, schools, districts, and parents all measure learning and student academic growth by multiple forms of testing and assessment procedures, but character traits aren't measurable on standardized tests. Our lessons and instruction must include real-life challenges and situations because the world is looking for people who know their skills and get along well with other people.

Authentic assessment asks students to demonstrate knowledge learned by use of real-world activities and examples. Performance assessment requires students to demonstrate knowledge and skills learned through recalling information, for example: assignments, tests, essays, presentations, journals, and questions in the back of chapters. Portfolios are collections of student work over time that show evidence of learning and progress. Portfolios require a large amount of storage space but can be used both as authentic and performance assessment tools.

The classroom assessment process is a teacher goal to improve student learning and provide feedback for instructional effectiveness. A teacher should include self-assessment practices so that students are able to examine and evaluate their own work and be clear thinkers and achieve higher expectations.

Part Two

The "Trade Secrets" of Classroom Management

Introduction

My congratulations to all teachers who are sincere and understanding and who create exciting instructional lessons and activities for students. I am fortunate to be acquainted with many outstanding educators who have their "heart and soul" in teaching and connect with their students. We as teachers know classroom management is a skill that is not only learned but should be practiced daily.

Teachers, new or experienced, share difficulties working with children; they would probably respond with discipline and student achievement. Learning requires discipline! Classroom management becomes successful with establishing respect, trust, and a system of values that leads each student to develop self-discipline, responsibility, and direction.

Teachers are aware of these main categories in taking action for discipline problems: proactive, reactive, and intervention.

1. Proactive:
   These are actions taken to reduce the number of problems before they arise. Teachers who provide an interesting instructional program, active learning environment, and work with students on developing self-discipline and responsibility have a higher success rate with positive behavior with students.
2. Reactive:

These are actions taken when students violate classroom, school, and district code of conduct. It is critical to address the problems immediately so that issues will not escalate and intervention strategies are needed.

3. Intervention:
    These are actions taken when a student's behavior is very serious and simple reactive practices will not maintain safety or learning.

The ideal situation is to encourage proactive methods in the classroom for reinforcement and to use simple and effective consequences as preventive measures.

Most students have a keen sense of fair play. They also are able to assess your classroom environment and realize what they can and can't do. There are a number of programs to help teachers establish a proactive climate regarding discipline and non-confrontational, logical ways of reacting when problems do arise. Programs such as Developing Capable People, Capturing Kids' Hearts, Love and Logic, Positive Discipline, and Discipline with Dignity are a few. All have at their core, either explicitly stated or implied, the following elements:

1. Building perceptions of capability or success.
2. Building perceptions of importance or significance.

3. Building perceptions that allow students to make decisions and experience consequences.
4. Building an environment of consistency.
5. Building mutually respectful relationships.

The destination for educational planning reveals a main highway of thinking and attitudes that will provide teachers and staff with ideas that reinforce planning and good classroom management, which is half the battle in discipline. Let us discover the "trade secrets" of classroom discipline, management, routines, procedures, positive behavior, and self-discipline.

Consistency + Follow-through = Security: Establish Positive Routines and Procedures

Positive Routines

1. Encourage *success* as a motivator.
2. Develop perception of *importance*.
3. Know your *decisions* and consequences.
4. *Consistency* + Follow-through = Security
5. Build *respect* and trust.

Success in a school is a strong motivator to prevent improper behavior. The balance between creating opportunities for challenges and successes is a teacher's awareness that different students require various amounts of success to stay motivated. At-risk students need to be motivated the majority of time, and the very talented students experience success half of the time. Just a reminder, extended periods of failure would break anyone's optimism. Teachers, check how active your strategic and long-range plans are involving your students in the learning environment.

Encourage success as a motivator.

1. Basics to challenges
   Spending time on basic skills and knowledge and then moving to a higher level of

thinking will result in reasonable challenges and successes for students.

2. Questions

   Questions should cover the basic skills, and modify them to challenge the advanced students.

3. Recognition

   Recognizing students who are successful in other areas of school is essential because not everyone is capable at everything. Good judgment on our part and common sense will motivate, rescue, and allow mistakes as learning lessons.

4. Direct instruction and master skills

   All students and especially at-risk students must begin with small portions of information before there is understanding. As a next step, competent students take in and comprehend larger amounts of information.

Develop perception of *importance*.

1. Recognize

   All students should feel that they have purpose and important roles in the school community. As teachers, if we miss opportunities to recognize and reinforce each student's accomplishments and encourage their involvement in school life, we increase behavioral problems.

2. Contribute

   Students need to feel they are making a contribution and there is a sense of belonging; encourage them to be part of a group, club, sports team, or organization. These contributions will help decrease behavioral issues before they begin and offer students positive activities.

3. Perception of importance

   Teachers are instrumental in emphasizing the importance of each student by being good listeners, asking for student help when needed, and offering classroom jobs. Giving students time to meet in groups to discuss classroom ideas and activities is invaluable for a perception of importance.

Know your *decisions* and consequences.

1. Decisions and consequences

   Consequences that do not fit the rules or goals cause students to retreat, rebel, or seek revenge. Students who have time to reflect on their individual problems also have opportunities to learn.

2. Decision-making power

   Students do learn from positive decisions and consequences when they preserve the dignity of the student. Reflection helps to think about his or her thinking, reactions, and what could have been different.

Class rules can be a collaboration between teachers and students. If everyone knows the boundaries and there is a decision-making process within boundaries, then behavior problems are at a minimum.

Consistency + Follow-through = Security

1. Classrooms without surprises
    Teachers who establish consistent routines in their classroom's management, lesson plans, and activities experience fewer discipline problems. Students should be well aware of all rules, consequences, and experience few surprises. The challenge for teachers is offering a change in the curriculum, either using an alternate lesson or from your "bag of tricks" that doesn't create big surprises. Consistency is essential!

2. Consistency practices

    a. Establish beginning of the day, ending of the day, and overall classroom routines.
    b. Establish and follow a set of rules, expectations, and consequences.
    c. Follow school and district discipline guidelines.
    d. Resolve discipline matters as soon as possible.
    e. Follow your daily, short, and long-range plans.
    f. Stay emotionally neutral and calm.

Build *respect* and trust.

1. Respect

    Respect is a character quality needed by all humans. We have a chance to enhance a student's attitude, thinking, and behavior with continued examples of respect and dignity. Teachers, you have the awesome and joyful treat to unlock the "heart and soul" of education for yourself and your students. Move ahead and make those connections.

2. Dignity

    Dignity is the key to earning a student's respect. How would we as teachers want to be treated by our colleagues? These are several examples:

    1.provide the correct example for a wrong answer, reducing embarrassment;

    2.encourage students to seek the correct answers;

    3.discussing a problem in private reinforces respect and dignity—not embarrassing a student in front of their peers.

The bottom line is that preserving a student's dignity is a giant step to developing a strong relationship between teachers and students and reduces discipline problems.

Positive Procedures

Even with good planning and an active learning atmosphere, real problems and mischief occur with a few, and students will test you. Minor concerns aren't likely to become major ones if each teacher remembers these following guidelines. I made a point to review these procedures and my management program throughout my teaching years. They were good reminders, especially at the beginning and several times during the school year. I know you will recognize these guidelines.

• • • • • • • • • • • •

Teacher Thinking, Attitudes, and Planning

1. Be the kind of teacher students will respect, trust, and consider fair.
2. Exude confidence and maintain your poise.
3. Be enthusiastic and keep a sense of humor. Enthusiasm is contagious.
4. Allow students to know that you care.
5. Being organized is an important trait for a teacher.
6. Maintain an attractive and orderly classroom.
7. Planning and good classroom management is half the battle in discipline.
8. Keep expectations high and overplan (remember your "bag of tricks" and alternate plans).

9. Make your lessons interesting, imaginative, and related to real-life situations.
10. Establish as few rules as possible, and keep them simple. Examine them regularly.
11. Other suggestions:

    a. Learn student names as soon as possible.
    b. Be firm, fair, and admit mistakes when you make them.
    c. Be consistent and follow-through.
    d. Show students what is important to them.

Teachers + Students = Success

1. Know your students individually and academically.
2. Remind yourself that everyone needs success stories, especially at-risk children.
3. Be consistent! Unacceptable behavior is always unacceptable.
4. Follow-through as soon as possible on resolving problems.
5. Do not punish the group for an individual's actions.
6. Do not make deals to obtain discipline.
7. Make an effort not to use assignments as a punishment.
8. Refuse to make threats or humiliate a student.
9. Encounter each student with discussion about a problem and avoid arguing.

10. Handle the "normal" behavioral issues yourself, but for those more difficult concerns, seek the skills of a specialist.

11. Look for the positive or "Catch the student doing something right." Begin fresh everyday! This does not mean you forget all previous infractions; it does mean you begin your teaching day with the expectation that students will be on task, listen, follow directions, and behave positively.

Students learn in an atmosphere that is organized and attention is given to the lesson, skill, activity, or subject matter at hand. The teacher must have well-prepared lessons to know exactly how long to spend on each lesson part so that students are not left without anything to do. If a student causes a disturbance while you are teaching—for example: talks out, makes noises, bangs a pen, gives remarks about the lesson—he or she needs to be stopped immediately. These are practical suggestions that all teachers will recognize in their classes.

What are some procedures to alter negative behavior?

1. Stop teaching in the middle of a sentence when there is noise in the room. Look at those noisy students.

2. Involve students in the entire lesson discussion and activities. You will notice if they are paying attention, and you will keep them alert.

3. Develop a sense of timing for when it is time to change activities.
4. Write a student's name on the board to see him or her at break or lunch. Some students test you to see how far they can go and want to see if you will get excited and yell.
5. Escort a student who is out of control to the office for attracting the attention of the class. This is a last resort because attention and learning by the class is impossible under these circumstances.

What are some techniques for helping lessons and activities move forward?

1. Write the directions on the board, explain the directions, and have several students repeat directions for clarity.
2. Go to students for answering questions.
3. Motivate students to stop work. For example: Say, "We have two more minutes," when you want them to stop, then have them move quietly and quickly.
4. Allow students to have a routine and specific time to sharpen pencils, throw paper away, get a book, or any other privilege or need.
5. Pass materials and papers row to row by selecting several students. The same procedure holds for clean-up.

What are some practical suggestions?

1. Assign definite seats to specific students.
2. Take time to have a student verbalize the situation or problem in private.

    a. What exactly did you do?
    b. What were you supposed to be doing?
    c. What could you do to make up for this problem? (A student will need guidance.)

3. Handle each student's situation differently.
4. Relate to cultural, individual, backgrounds, and home life to understand problems.
5. Find something to praise in every student.

> Dear Mr. Grossi,
>
>   Thank you so much for what you have done for me and being an awesome teacher for the last three years. I have learned so much about grammar, writing, study habits, time management, and how to get along better with others because I was talkative and active. But thanks to your persistence, being firm, and patience, I understood what it means to be a good listener and quiet myself. Anyway, you did a great job dealing with me. I hope that you will never forget me and the years that we had together.
>
>   Love,
>   —Laura Blanchard (eighth grade student)

Reflection: The importance of being more open to life and see the many talents and beauty of others are gifts that can be shared daily.

Dear Mr. Grossi,

Thank you for teaching me in the past year. I have learned much about life, grammar, writing, and the beauty of literature. You have guided me through all the small and large problems that I had during my first year of high school. I was a real pain in the neck, and we did have our challenges, but you never let up on me, and I feel I am a better person for it. You would always try to help solve our problems and made us laugh. I will never forget you. You are not only a good teacher, but a good friend.

Sincerely,
—Alex Bedrosian (ninth grade student)

Reflection: Students who are open to learning through knowledge discover more about life. Teachers, appreciate patience and be open to ways of dealing with conflicts and resolutions in a positive manner.

Discipline "Trade Secrets": Styles and Plans

Introduction

What is your discipline plan? Classroom management and discipline are an ongoing and difficult challenge for both teachers and parents. When you receive the correct advice, it can be reassuring and instructive. It is not necessary to select one discipline plan, but you may select aspects of several plans and different styles. Teachers may have similar approaches to discipline, but finding a philosophy that is different, works well, and fits your personal style of teaching is rewarding.

There are many "trade secrets" in classroom management and discipline. Your personal management plan should be an "open book," ready to make deletions, expand, and accept changes. Those "trade secrets" are your working standards and should suit your personality, instructional methods, and students.

Are you taking proactive measures to secure your classroom management program and create a positive teaching and learning environment? Each school may have different discipline plans for teachers to follow. Students need guidelines! They must buy into the plan and rules; and if you provide ways for them to have ownership in the decision-making process, there will be a stronger respect for those procedures. No matter what plan you use, consider these steps:

1. Teach the plan.
2. Practice and model the plan.
3. Be fair and consistent.
4. Follow through with rewards and consequences.

Consistency + Follow-through = Security

What are your proactive (preventive) measures? In order to have a consistent and working classroom management program, these are four major areas to consider:

1. Manage physical and psychological situations.
2. Manage instruction, time, and students.
3. Use a variety of teaching techniques and encouragement.
4. Establish an atmosphere and routines with respect, trust, and consistency.

The physical environment refers to the shape, size, desk arrangement, materials, and equipment in the classroom. The psychological environment is the tone and atmosphere of the classroom. The bottom line is your room should be organized, functional, and routines should flow throughout the school day.

Your classroom procedures should be clear to students so they are able to focus on learning. Your vision, goals, objectives, and outcomes are a daily reminder of your long-term plans. As a teacher, you are constantly "on stage" every day of the school year. This can be draining when you are asked to change with the times, be accountable, and told about the need for continuous improvement. It is easy to see how a teacher may lose enthusiasm for teaching. Always look for ways to reignite the original interests that first attracted you to the profession.

Are you regularly reviewing your teaching approaches, plans, and delivery? Your voice level, interest, delivery (face, eye, body movement), and application of proven teaching strategies will hold student interest. Students learn more effectively in a safe, validated, and positive environment. A teacher's job is to provide that type of atmosphere. Remind yourself of these strategies for teaching and creating more student successes: vary your instructional methods, encourage all students when appropriate, and apply a variety of teaching approaches.

When you have established routines, procedures, and expectations the first day and week, communicate and model them on a regular basis. Be sure you are comfortable with your classroom management program and hold students accountable for established procedures.

1. Management routines
   When transitions occur in the classroom—entering, leaving, distributing, collecting, activities, or changing classes—signals and directions are effective for students.
2. Activity routines
   The kinds of activities should have clear directions: location, time, and participation.

3. Instructional routines
   The teacher has a set pattern of actions and behaviors which alerts students that something is about to happen. This encompasses teaching planning routines.

Discipline Styles

The correct expert advice can be instructive and reassuring. It is just a matter of finding the one style or aspects of different discipline plans that fits your personality and situation and class dynamic. The following are a few of the popular plans among the many teachers have adapted for their classrooms. These are only summaries of the programs; please take the time to research and investigate these approaches for yourself.

Assertive Discipline Style (Lee Canter)

Lee Canter is well known for his "Assertive Discipline Program," published in *Educational Weekly*, 05/07/08. His style is available in many books, articles, and used by many teachers for the classroom.

Mr. Canter proposes a clear, firm, and calm method to preserve the expectations of the classroom. The assertive discipline plan consists of three major sections: rules, recognition, and consequences. Suggestions for rules are consistency, clear expectations, limited number of rules, and to observe behaviors in progress. He proposes for recognition the reinforcement of encouraging good behavior, positive environment, increase self-esteem, praise, and rewards. Teachers encourage and praise students for good behavior and follow-up the class expectations by recognition, home phone calls, and rewards. These are two sample plans that are summaries of the most used rules and plans from teacher friends and schools:

Sample Elementary Plan
Classroom Rules

1. Follow directions.
2. The Code of Conduct is based on the three R's: respect, responsibility, and relating to others.
3. Focus on the positive.

Recognition

1. Praise and recognition
2. Follow the classroom expectations
3. Positive notes on progress for students and sent home to parents

Consequences

1. First time: warning and discussion
2. Second time: conferences and written note
3. Third time: call parent and conference
4. Fourth time: send to the principal
5. Severe: send to the principal

Sample Secondary Plan
Classroom Rules

1. Follow directions and listen carefully
2. Be in the classroom and seated when the bell rings.
3. Do not swear

Recognition

1. Praise and recognition
2. Positive notes on progress for students and sent home to parents
3. Pass or other rewards

Consequences

1. First time: warning and discussion
2. Second time: privilege(s) denied
3. Third time: call parent and conference
4. Fourth time: send to the principal
5. Severe: send to the principal

After you have established your discipline plan, it is time to create a lesson plan to prepare and teach students why we have rules and consequences, use students as models, post the discipline plan in the classroom, and send a copy home for parents. The use of repetition, reinforcement, encouragement, and praise will help students support the class expectations throughout the school year. When a student chooses to disrupt the class, the consequence must be consistent and applied in a firm and calm manner. After the consequence is completed, wipe the slate clean, find something positive to say, and get the student back on track.

Discipline with Dignity

This flexible approach was adopted by Drs. Richard Curwin and Allen Mendler, authors of *Discipline with Dignity*. If you are interested in this popular style, please consult the many books, articles, the internet, and ASCD article, 1988, reprinted 1999 written on this program.

This discipline style is an effective approach for a school and the classroom. It emphasizes developing responsibility, right thinking, cooperation, respect, and shared decision-making at the onset of a problem. The teacher has the opportunity to help all students to learn long-term behavioral changes through values and consequences, not rewards and punishments.

Love and Logic Style

This discipline style was formed by Jim Fay for parents and teachers. This model teaches children and students responsible behavior through "love" and "logic." The key components are teaching children that actions have consequences and making the correct choices about their actions with intelligent thinking. Example of a love and logic statement: "I will be glad to talk to you about this when your voice is as calm as mine."

Discipline Philosophies

Evonne Lack wrote an article, "What's Your Discipline Style" in *Parent Center* magazine, last updated 05/07/08. She states that discipline is a tough challenge both for parents and teachers. Although the article is directed toward parents, the discipline styles are close to teachers and classroom management.

Boundary-Based Style (Limits and Consequences)

Students need boundaries to feel safe and secure. If students are not clear where the boundaries are, they will "test" until they experience or find them. Clearly communicate your rules and limits, and if there is a problem, make sure the consequence matches the behavior. Offer a choice; this will place the responsibility on the child.

Techniques: exploring choices together, cool-down and time-outs, and logical consequences

Example: A student talks out, makes remarks, and disturbs class learning. The teacher calmly asks the student to be quiet, and he or she refuses. Privately, "You can either choose to not blurt out comments, or we could select one of the consequences."

Gentle Discipline Style (Prevention and Diffusion)

The strategies that you plan to reduce opportunities for misbehavior are invaluable. When there is a problem, turn to diffusion and regular preventive techniques. See if there's an underlying problem, such as tiredness, boredom, hunger, being at a party last night, or something more serious. If not, turn to your "trade secrets," and use a distraction, redirect the student, validate any positive actions, or give him or her a choice.

Techniques: time-out, distraction, redirection, validation, and offer a choice.

Example: A student talks out, makes remarks, and disturbs class learning. The student has a cooling-off period and time-out to reflect and complete a form that offers a choice to make the situation right. A conference follows with redirection, validation, and follow-up.

Positive Discipline Style (Encouragement)

Students behave positively when they feel encouraged, have a sense of ownership, and feel they belong. Always chat with a student privately to find out the underlying cause for the misbehavior. Once you know the reason, offer the correct kind of encouragement, direct the child to work out a solution, and follow through with action. You have invested in another example of teaching respect and being responsible.

Techniques: positive time-outs, conference, consequences, and working together to find a solution.

Example: A student talks out, makes remarks, and disturbs class learning. The teacher says, "We have a problem; you are talking and disturbing the class. I think you can solve this. What do you think you should do?

Emotion Coaching Style (Communication and Recognition of Feelings)

When a student is able to recognize and understand their own feelings, they make better choices. The help you give in the style of discipline can strengthen the connection between the two of you. It is essential that you know your procedures and standards and what is acceptable behavior. If you are honest with the class and the child who has misbehaved, you might talk about feelings that are experienced in certain situations. The skill of empathy is valuable in these situations, and putting yourself in the child's shoes will reveal the "real feelings" behind the misbehavior. When there is understanding, trust develops.

Technique: identifying feelings, listening, and calm strategies

Example: A student talks out, makes remarks, and disturbs class learning. Privately, the teacher conferences with the student and acknowledges feelings and explains the behavior is not appropriate. Discussion and a natural consequence is administered.

Behavior Modification Style (Negative and Positive Reinforcement)

This discipline style is similar to the boundary base style and takes its roots from B. F. Skinner, an American psychologist. As a teacher, you emphasize clear expectations and limits and back them up with consequences. In behavior modification, you place emphasis on warnings and rewards.

Techniques: praise, rewards, consequences, time-outs, and warnings.

Example: A student talks out, makes remarks, and disturbs class learning. The student is asked firmly and calmly to stop the outbursts—this is your first warning. The student refuses—this is your second warning, etc.

The five descriptions of these discipline philosophies are brief and not the only styles available to educators. The boundary-based style does have consequences, and the gentle discipline style uses consequences; all of these styles overlap. Remember the differences are more a matter of what they emphasize, and a teacher needs to take the elements of any legitimate discipline plan and adapt it to his or her personality and teaching methods.

The Honor Level Style

"Discipline by Design," The Honor Level Systems, internet 05/11/08. Approximately fifteen states, including Canada and New Zealand, use the Honor Level style.

This discipline style was developed about twenty-five years ago from a school district in the state of Washington. It is a proactive approach dealing with student behaviors, and it has a combination of Assertive, Boundary, and Empathetic Base features which strongly encourages respect, trust, and responsibility. Parents, teachers, and administrators are involved in this program, and records are maintained of the various stages of recognition and disciplinary actions taken on each student.

1. Honor Level One (estimate: 70–80 percent of students)

    These are students who rarely get into trouble. They must not be in detention or sent for time-out for a period of fourteen days. The school plans special privileges and activities for these students; for example: extended lunch breaks, extra recreational periods, ice-cream, or special activity.

2. Honor Level Two (estimate: 20–30 percent of students)

    These students may have had several problems in the last fourteen days. It is possible for some students in this level to receive some extra privileges.

3. Honor Level Three (estimate: 5–10 percent of students)

    These students have more difficulty staying out of trouble. They will have three or more problems during the fourteen days and receive no extra privileges. Usually, detention and study hall are the places they make up time with appropriate consequences.

4. Honor Level Four (estimate: 3–5 percent of students)

These students are consistently in trouble and do not participate in any of the extra activities. They serve time in detention, study hall, or complete some community service at the school site.

The school takes into account the student's discipline record for the last fourteen days. There is always a way to work back to Honor Level One, and the emphasis is each day is a new day. Unfortunately, there are times when negative consequences are a part of behavior modification: sent to the office, parent conferences, suspension, and expulsion. Many schools have adopted this design but select their own elements to depict the school and staff personality.

Win-Win Discipline Style

This is a plan created by Dr. Spencer Kagan from Kagan Professional Development, *Kagan Online Magazine*, Winter 2002.

This approach is designed to handle discipline problems at the moment of disruption by getting to the root of the issue and taking care of a student's unfulfilled needs. He wants us to reflect on these three basic needs:

1. Students' needs are being met, and there are no apparent discipline problems.
2. Students' needs are not being met, and they are dealing with them responsibly.
3. Students' needs are not being met, and they act out and create discipline problems.

Dr. Kagan proposes that we meet each student's needs individually and offer them strategies that are respectful and responsible to deal with their unmet needs. Disruptive behavior fades away, and the student wins.

The Win-Win approach is based on the concept of "Positions":

1. Attention seeking
2. Avoiding embarrassment
3. Anger venting
4. Control seeking
5. Energetic
6. Bored
7. Uninformed

There are five components of the Win-Win discipline by five Ps:

1. Pillars (philosophy, expectations, and goals)
2. Procedures (procedures that prevent problems before they occur)
3. Positions (offers students non-disruptive ways to deal with needs)
4. Process (strategies for the moment of disruption and follow-ups)
5. Programs (use programs that prevent discipline problems)

The previous discipline styles mentioned are only some of the many behavioral programs that schools and teachers find successful within the educational community.

Whether you select specific sections or the entire discipline plan to combine and make your own, be sure that it is clear, fair, firm, productive, and students take ownership of the approach. This is a sample of some elements that could be included when you are writing a discipline program:

1. Know the difference between expected and unexpected behaviors.
2. Expect student achievement and successes.
3. Know the consequences, and be aware the steps are fair.
4. Expect a quick response and action.
5. Allow time for discussion and conferences.

6. Have a written policy that is workable and open for revisions.

Classroom Behaviors and Suggestions

Prevent Cheating

Cheating is a big concern for middle and high school students, and it is not uncommon for elementary school children. There are many pressures for students to do well in school, and cheating can become a regular occurrence. A teacher can be a strong influence in emphasizing the importance of honesty.

1. Talk privately with your class or with students.
2. Explain the rules before giving a test.
3. Change the room arrangement if necessary.
4. Give students different versions of the tests.
5. Monitor students while they are taking a test.
6. Arrange a parent conference for a student who has cheated.

Students Who "Bother" Their Classmates

Students "bother" their classmates in a variety of ways: poke, pull their hair, grab something, trip, push, call them names, interrupt, spread rumors, and ridicule them. The teacher needs to talk with the students involved to determine the conflict, what students may be blame-free, or observe the behavior before prescribing the punishment.

1. Check the student's concern before dismissing it.
2. Encourage the complaining student to assert him or herself.
3. Provide the student with a consequence.
4. Have a talk with the student or students.
5. Decide what is motivating the students.
6. Move the student desk.
7. Restrict the student's physical contact with specific classmates.
8. Find ways to give positive attention.

The Backtalker

A student who is disrespectful to a teacher makes it difficult to conduct a lesson.

The teacher needs to realize that it is not related to what you said or did. Keeping calm in the face of a student's verbal assault isn't easy. What you can do?

1. Don't take it personally.
2. Calmly inform the student that the language is inappropriate.
3. Have a private talk with the student.
4. Explain to the student that the behavior is disrespectful.
5. Document the student's comments.
6. Select a consequence that fits the behavior.

7. If the behavior happens a second time, arrange a parent conference.

Homework Help

Homework is a frequent source of problems for the teacher and student. Teachers assign homework to reinforce skills learned and provide opportunities for children to become independent learners. The challenge for teachers is to encourage students to take homework seriously and realize it is the student's responsibility.

1. Communicate your homework policy to parents.
2. Write assignments on the board, use the telephone, and make use of the internet.
3. Have students begin homework at the end of class.
4. Reward students an activity when all assignments are completed.
5. Establish an assignment folder for each student.
6. Have students complete missing homework form.
7. Assign homework to students' needs, if necessary.

Minor Behaviors and Consequences

First Offense Minimum of two or three day detention

Second Offense Conference with principal, counselor and/or parent and five day detention

Third Offense Minimum of five days detention or school service work

Fourth Offense Minimum of five days detention, school service work, and dropped from sports and other activities for a time period.

Fifth Offense Possible suspension from one to five days

1. Bullying, teasing, pestering, or tormenting another student.
2. Disrespectful to a student, teacher, or employee.
3. Disrespectful language or conduct.
4. Truancy: absent from school without the authority of the parents or the school.
5. Repeated minor offenses; ongoing problems.

Major Behaviors and Consequences

First Offense Referral to the counselor, principal, and/or notify the parent about the situation. Minimum five-day detention.

Second Offense Minimum five-day detention and school service work.

Possible suspension or expulsion depending upon the severity of the problem.

Third Offense Ten-day detention and possible recommendation for suspension or expulsion.

Fourth Offense Recommendation of suspension or expulsion up to twelve months.

1. Trespassing
2. Threats of physical aggression
3. Use or possession of tobacco
4. Extortion or blackmail
5. Gross teacher disrespect (use of vulgar or profane language)
6. Profanity and vulgarity (decided case-by-case)

First Offense Minimum five-day detention and referral to the counselor, principal, and notify the parent about the situation. Restitution.

Second Offense Minimum ten-day detention and recommendation of suspension or expulsion. Law enforcement will be contacted.

1. Breaking and entering
2. Assault on a staff member or volunteer
3. False fire alarms
4. Selling, using, distributing drugs or other substances
5. Vandalism
6. Possession of a dangerous weapon (expulsion and call law enforcement)

The student needs to:

1. Identify the problem he or she created.
2. Identify the problem created for others, and make restitution.
3. Recognize what is the underlying problem (guidance).
4. Analyze the behavior and how it affected others.
5. Complete a discipline form or write a letter explaining how he or she felt about the situation before, during, and after the problem was created.
6. Make a written plan outlining the action taken to prevent a similar situation from happening again.
7. Arrange an appointment with the teacher, counselor, or principal to discuss the plan.

Self-discipline and Growth

Introduction

The Little Prince by Antoine Saint-Exupery is a short and simple book that shares the important messages of experiencing challenges, love, respect, responsibility, and successes. The second part of the book contains a very profound definition of friendship. You only are able to encourage more success stories if you know each person as an individual and student. There is a part that begins with the Little Prince and a fox, and the fox asks the Little Prince to "tame" him. Excerpt's taken from "The Little Prince."

> Fox: Good morning, said the fox.
> Little Prince: Good morning, said the Little Prince.
> Fox: I am right here under the apple tree.
> Little Prince: Who are you?
> Fox: I am a fox.
> Little Prince: Come and play with me.
> Fox: I cannot play with you. I am not tamed.
> Little Prince: What do you mean, I am not tamed?
> Fox: Who are you really looking for?
> Little Prince: I am looking for friends. What does that mean … to tame?
> Fox: It is an act too often neglected. It means to establish ties.
> Little Prince: To establish ties?
> Fox: The fox gazed at the Little Prince for a long time! Please, tame me!
> Little Prince: I want to, very much. But I have not

much time. I have friends to   discover and a great many things to understand.

Fox: One only understands the things that one tames, said the fox.

Little Prince: What must I do to tame you? asked the Little Prince.

Fox: You must be very patient, replied the fox.

The fox and the Little Prince continued their conversation, and eventually the Little Prince tamed the fox. They extended their farewells, and the fox offered him this one last important message.

> And now here is my secret, a very simple secret: it is only with the heart that one can see rightly; what is essential is invisible to the eye. The Little Prince repeated each response to be sure to remember. For example, the time you have spent on your rose, makes your rose so important. You become responsible forever, for whatever you have tamed.
>
> *The Little Prince* by Antoine Saint-Exupery

You do not know how special someone is until you bind your heart to him or her. In other words, you do not know a person's specialness or their role in life until you "establish ties." Therefore, taming can be defined as creating a bond or building a bridge between yourself and someone else.

Just as the fox taught the Little Prince a lesson about "taming" and "establishing ties," we as educators must encourage self-discipline and success stories within our students. Yes, the acts of teaching, creating a vision, sharing knowledge, knowing the student's gifts, and encouraging student accomplishments are not easy tasks today. We can only hope for the best and know we are doing the best jobs possible.

What is hope? Hope takes never ceasing to be amazed, wearing your soul on your sleeve, holding your breath, but most of all believing that you'll make a difference and that each person matters. So, when you begin your planning and preparation to create success stories for students in your classroom, just remember to provide them with many opportunities to understand positive behavior, enjoy positive behavior, and practice positive behavior.

What Is Positive Behavior?

Self-discipline is all about self-control and responsibility for one's desires and actions. Children will become self-disciplined by practicing positive behaviors in small ways; thereby, this will help them in big ways when they are adults. Teachers and parents want children to take the initiative and demonstrate leadership skills. If students cannot lead themselves in and out of the school environment, they cannot lead others.

Personal organization will demonstrate how a student categorizes things, and this is a sign of how organized they are. If you develop and practice an organizational system with students, they will strengthen their time management skills.

Responsibility is a key concept for positive behavior. If a student has a habit of blaming others or has difficulty accepting responsibility for his or her actions, this will limit the growth of self-discipline. Being responsible is a positive quality and mistakes made are not to be looked at as negative, as long as a student learns from them.

Accountability is a characteristic that determines what kind of person a student will be. What they do in life, the kinds of friends they make, and personal values for themselves on a daily basis will affect their future.

Child psychologist Haim Ginott wrote these thoughts about the role of teachers in the classroom. Teachers are not only successful having a clear vision, planning, and positive atmosphere but more with an enthusiasm for the subjects and respect for their students. Let's make connections to the "heart and soul' of teaching and students' growth in self-discipline.

> "I have come to a frightening conclusion. I am the decisive element in the classroom. It is my personal approach that creates the climate. It is my daily mood that makes the weather. As a teacher, I possess tremendous power to make a child's life miserable or joyous. I can be a tool of torture or an inspiration. I can humiliate or humor, hurt or heal. In all situations, it is my response that decides whether a crisis will be escalated or de-escalated, and a child humanized or de-humanized." (National Education Association Magazine, Classroom Management, 02/18/08)

When teachers take the time to know their students as individuals, it is an effective strategy to promote positive discipline. These positive relationships offer the groundwork for other strategies, including listening, responding to rules and requests, and becoming more respectful of others. These are some suggestions to encourage positive behaviors:

1. Demonstrate your interest in each student (listen to them and remember what they say).
2. Praise the continuation of appropriate behaviors.
3. Show interest in helping students.
4. Explain the purpose of rules.
5. Encourage students to participate in class and school activities.

How Can Students Enjoy Positive Behavior?

Teachers face the same challenges of managing their students' behavior and teaching the curriculum. There are so many conflicting theories on how to manage your class and provide logical consequences and assertive discipline. It is critical for every teacher to begin with a solid and clear classroom management program. I have taken the time to interview teachers, read about discipline plans, and visit classrooms over the last twenty-five years.

It has been a real education for me to see educators using their own discipline programs and taking the best of each program and adapting it for my class-room. In my observations, I noted there are numerous classroom management styles. These are the suggestions that seemed to appear most often for positive classroom management.

1. Make your strategies clear and you lead your class confidently and effectively.
2. Review your strategies on a regular basis, and they will help you to face any challenges.
3. Make sure classroom rules, expectations, and consequences are positive and concise.
4. Remind yourself that when you model, you let students know you follow your own rules.
5. Praise and encourage students who are trying and struggling.
6. Show respect and listen carefully to their successes and needs.
7. Consistency + Follow-through + Praise = Security
8. Provide appropriate assignments and activities at the ability levels of each student.
9. Have students take ownership in the class by making suggestions for the rules and consequences. Students react more positively when they help create the rules.

We are all aware that creating an atmosphere and environment in which students know and follow rules is challenging, but not impossible. You can lay a solid foundation for student growth in respect, responsibility, and self-discipline that lasts all year.

What Does It Mean to Practice Positive Behavior?

Skills of self-discipline and responsibility are formed in the home with the help of parents, along with other positive characteristics. Schools and teachers are partners with the home in forming each child as a person and a student. Teachers, effective classroom management involves all the qualities mentioned in parts one and two of this book. I want to emphasize that a teacher's attitude, enthusiasm, expectations, and positive action will improve classroom behavior and social skills. Remember: Consistency + Follow-through + Praise = Security. Creating a positive learning atmosphere, using caring reinforcement to encourage positive behavior, looking for positive behaviors instead of misbehaviors will only produce positive student feedback. What are some common reinforcement techniques? Teaching children with social and self-management skills can eliminate inappropriate behavior and increase student learning. Social skills are person-to-person communications that involve giving, receiving, and listening carefully. Students who lack social behavior skills lack adult models, or learning opportunities, or may have emotional disturbances that interfere with social interaction with other people.

Students must be taught to view their problem from a different perspective and find possible solutions that are fair, safe, and effective. It is important to include listening, looking at the person, clarifying meaning, and making appropriate responses to the person.

Self-management skills include having positive attitudes and behaviors, the ability to set and achieve goals, and possessing a positive attitude toward changes. Teaching self-management skills develops responsibility and teaches students to take an active role in the discipline plan. Examples:

1. Identify the behavior to be changed by teacher and students.
2. Identify when and where the negative behavior frequently occurs.
3. Set realistic goals for students for changing the behavior.
4. Set a time line for reviewing progress.
5. Identify the effective reinforcement and consequence.
6. Complete self-evaluations by students to determine successes and needs.

Classroom management programs and discipline plans vary from class to class because of a teacher's personal styles and characteristics of students. An effective classroom behavior management is planned with a set of rules, consequences, positive feedback, and consistency. Consistency + Follow-through + Praise = Security.

Tips from Veteran Teachers

Teacher Vision Magazine, "Behavior Management Tips from Veteran Teachers," Teaching Methods, 04/22/08 (internet).

1. Have a good balance of discipline and humor with children.

> "In order to gain respect, you need to convey your genuine enjoyment being with them. My students understand I am sometimes tough on them because I care enough to wish they would try harder and get better. I also manage to find a way to show I care in a meaningful way. Humor is important to have for your own perspective and for the children. It keeps the day lively and enjoyable."
> —Georgene Asseiri, Phoenix, Arizona,
> grades K-2

2. Children will quiet down when the teacher is quiet and waiting for attention.

> "I lost my voice the first year trying to focus their attention on me. Now, I simply wait for the attention I deserve before moving on to the next lesson or set of instructions. It really works."
> —Cecilia Martinez, Sylmar, California,
> grades 3–5

3. Adolescents love choices and challenges!

> "Whenever possible give students choices—whether it's a long-range project on a country or coloring a map with crayons, marker, or colored pencils. I try

to give as many small choices as possible, even if it seems insignificant."
—Sergio Chavez, Ayer Middle School, Ayer, Maryland, grades 6–8

4. Examine your classroom carefully for the best traffic patterns.

"Even if you have a custodian move a "permanent" fixture such as a pencil sharpener mounted on a wall, arrange traffic patterns so students may get out of their seats to take care of business (sharpen pencils, turn in work, etc.) without walking through areas where students are working. I have found this works well to keep potential mischief makers in check at the high school level where students are a bit old to ask permission every time they need "to blow their nose."
—Charmaine Wierzbicki, Calumet High School, Gary, Indiana.

Awards, Recognition, and Recognition Ideas

What are some reasons for offering rewards and recognition for students?

1. To reinforce desired behaviors.
2. To acknowledge a special accomplishment.
3. To recognize good attendance.
4. To reinforce leadership and teamwork.
5. To acknowledge improvement.
6. To build student confidence.
7. To recognize academic achievement.

What are some strategies to recognize students?

1. Postcards and letters to students and parents.
2. Wall of fame
3. Certificates
4. Birthday surprises, free homework pass, pen, pencil, or eraser
5. Students of the month
6. Student suggestion box
7. Honor roll
8. Free choice activity and/or food treats

• • • • • • • • • • • • • •

Name _____ Grade ___ Time ___
Date _____

1. Please review this communication record with your son or daughter.
2. This record indicates one or more problem situations that have occurred recently.
3. Return this form with the appropriate signatures by the date due stated below.
4. Your prompt attention and cooperation to this matter is appreciated.

____Shows lack of respect
　　___ students
　　___ teachers/staff
____Defiance of authority
____Disruption of classroom

instruction and teaching

_____Using vulgar/obscene language

_____Harassment of students

_____Threatening students

_____Bullying

_____Fighting or "play fighting"

_____Defacing school property

_____   Stealing

_____   Lying

_____   Cheating

_____   Does not conform to _____

_____   Classwork

_____   Homework

_____   Inconsistent performance

_____   Needs to follow directions

_____   Lack of attention

_____   Does not use time wisely

_____   Must improve study habits

_____   Incomplete work

_____   Late work

_____   Missing work

Month of: _____

_____   Too many absences: # _____

_____   Too many tardies: # _____

_____   Overall behavior must improve

_____   Overall academics must improve

Other: _____

___Conference required
   ___ Teacher/Student
   ___ Parent/Teacher
   ___ Parent/Principal/Teacher

___ Detention with instructions
   ___ In-school
   ___ Outside of school
   ___ Probable suspension

Other: _____
This form is due back by: _____
Teacher/Principal signature: _____
Date: _____

Parent signature: _____
Date: _____

Student signature: _____
Date: _____
Office copy: white Faculty copy: yellow Parent copy: pink

Dear Mr. Grossi,

Well, how is it going? I wanted to thank you for all you have done for me and my class these past two years. If it weren't for you, I don't think any of us in our class would be where we are now. You were firm, kept the rules, and brought out the good in everyone in our class. You showed us our strengths, and taught us how to improve our weaknesses. You also mean a lot to the rest of the school. Being the sixth grade teacher, student council moderator, and in charge of the school concerts is way too much. Before you were here, all the concerts were boring. I think you have been a better student council moderator than our class has ever seen. You were so very active in the council, even when you had little talent to work with. You were also a great teacher. You are the best teacher we had. I want to thank you, and the rest of the class will miss you.

Thank you,
—Danny Chase (sixth grade student)

Dear Mr. Grossi,

They say in your life you will meet one teacher who will change your life. This saying is true. They also say that this teacher will come in high school. In this case it's not true. You have been not only my favorite teacher, but also my friend, mentor, role model, and inspiration.

You helped me discover two talents I never knew I had—those talents are acting and being a good student. In the seventh grade, I thought I didn't have any talent at all. However, by the end of the year, there is no way I can express all my gratitude for you. Please keep in touch and remember leader that you will always be my favorite teacher. Thank you.

Love always,
—Erin Schmidt (seventh grade student)

Dear Mr. Grossi,

I hate having to tell you good-bye and move on to another grade. You have helped our class grow and mature. We learned a great deal thanks to your knowledge, your patience, and your caring ways. We entered sixth grade feeling insecure and with a reputation, if you know what I mean. In no time you improved our student skills and our self-esteem, and you made learning fun. You made us think, you made us laugh, you treated us with respect and love. For you, we did our plays, danced the tango and jitterbug, and who can forget the Chorus Line. We will see you at graduation. Thank you Mr. Grossi, you have been a great teacher and a great motivator, I will miss you.

Love,
—Michelle Tan (sixth grade student)

Dear G. Man,

From here on is honesty and nothing else. On the first day of school last year, I thought you were gonna (sic) be another one of those boring teachers. After a couple of weeks into the new year, my friend George and I began to realize that you were different, and actually had a quality unlike any teacher at that time.

George and I finally found a teacher who cared and understood what adolescent punk-rock, non-conformist kids felt like, and you would listen and understand us. We could talk to you about rock, girls, friendships, and any problems. Also, you accepted us for who we are. Thanks for everything: the good study habits, making class fun, and the great social studies lessons.

Love,
—Matt and George

Summary: Part Two

Don't ever try to understand everything—some things will never make sense.
Don't ever be reluctant to show your feelings—when you are happy give in to it.
Don't ever be afraid to try to make things better—you might be surprised at the results.
Don't ever take the weight of the world on your shoulders or be threatened by the future: take life one day at a time.
Don't ever feel guilty about the past—what's done is done, learn from your mistakes.
Don't ever feel alone—there is always someone there for you.
Don't forget that you can achieve what you imagine.
Don't ever stop believing and dreaming your dreams.

> —Poem and reading by Laine Parsons

What wonderful personal goals for both teachers and students to achieve beyond subjects and facts.

Part Three

Turn on the Lights of Success

Introduction

See the Invisible

"A teacher's ability to relate to students and to make positive, caring connections with them plays a significant role in cultivating a positive learning environment and promoting student achievement."
—James H. Stronge, author of *Qualities of Effective Teachers*

A Supportive Classroom Environment

Teachers are fortunate to have many strategies available to create an inviting, respectful, and supportive classroom environment.

Heterogeneous groups provide opportunities for students to learn and work together with a variety of students. It is essential to develop groupings that go beyond gender, racial, ethnic, and disability boundaries. To ensure success, students need to know the following: size of the group, directions, procedures, and expectations.

Group size whether the group is small or large dictates the task, assignment, or project. You may have a small group for a definite task all year long and occasional large group projects.

Student identities offer a way to get to know one another: style of working, personality, leadership, and talents help to create more successes in learning.

Classroom traditions provide a sense of belonging

to the class and include activities and experiences that are unique to the students.

Celebrations acknowledge accomplishments, efforts, and achievements. They take time, planning, and preparation for promoting identity and connections with the students.

A Success-Oriented Instructional Program

Teachers, have you reviewed your vision, goals, and objectives in reference to your overall strategic plans for the school year? Do you have a positive attitude and enthusiasm in planning your classroom curriculum and management program? What does your classroom environment look like? Are students involved in learning? Our lives are changing so rapidly in the twenty-first century that the knowledge we share must not only cover every subject area but focus on skills and abilities to manage, process, and understand information. These are some thoughts for yourself and your students:

1. Convey content and information that students can use in and out of the classroom.
2. Think about the "what" and the "why" of teaching.
3. Use technology, and model the importance of its use in the classroom.
4. Reinforce the qualities of respect, responsibility, trust, and collaboration with others.

5. Plan ongoing professional development for yourself.
6. Plan and maintain support systems that will help you professionally.
7. Use your "bag of tricks," and alternate plans to promote student interest in learning.
8. Use assessment and evaluation tools to help review your goals and objectives and offer time for self-evaluation of your teaching, lessons, and student learning.

Believe in the Impossible

When we think of a flexible classroom curriculum, a variety of perspectives on learning and active instructional strategies come to mind. We all realize that not everyone learns in the same way. Some are visual; others need to hear and verbalize. There are kinesthetic learners, other students prefer working alone, and some like small group interaction. If you believe that the impossible can truly be possible for you as a teacher and your students, it will produce successful surprises. Your flexible classroom curriculum allows students to take responsibility for their own learning, and as a teacher, you become a facilitator of knowledge. These are some benefits of active learning:

1. Allows students to be recognized for special strengths.
2. Provides opportunities for students to adapt their learning styles to their interests.

3. Reduces the chance of boredom by increasing the variety of activities.
4. Promotes teaching methods and student learning styles that work successfully.

Achieve the Incredible

A success-oriented classroom atmosphere is as important as the content and skills learned by students. If you travel the halls of an elementary, middle, or high school, it becomes obvious what classrooms are "electric," exciting, and teaching at "full speed ahead." Motivation, self-esteem growth, and morale building inspire students to be active learners and know that their teachers are ready for action, have goals and objectives, and things are happening instead of to happen. Achieve the incredible by being prepared, and "fire-up" your students to achieve!

See the Invisible: A Solid Education for Students

Introduction

Does your classroom environment need a "shot in the arm," a change, or revamping? Or, is your classroom atmosphere an inviting place but needs a jolt to enhance your vision? We have already shared that a solid education for students encourages social interaction, active learning, and self-motivation.

Celebrate the successes attained because it serves to reward effort, acknowledge hard work, motivate students, and build self-esteem. When teachers celebrate with students, it builds teamwork and rapport. These perceptions will build productive persons in society and create a desire to achieve. This chapter will concentrate on suggestions, ideas, and programs that create a supportive and success-oriented classroom environment.

Supportive Classroom Characteristics

There are various qualities of the classroom environment that we as teachers need to create so both students and teachers are comfortable and learn together. As the teacher, you are the role model and own the responsibility as the primary leader in your classroom.

1. The classroom must be a *safe place*.
    The teacher must make the classroom safe physically and emotionally. A safe place does not mean there is no accountability or difficult situations, but it is a fair and respectful environment.
2. The classroom must have times of *celebration*.
    School is not easy for many students, and times of celebration for individuals and the class are important. The results are building of teamwork, loyalty, and unity.
3. The teacher must have *high expectations*.
    Students will rise to realistic and high

expectations. You have to support their journey, and that means crying with them, laughing, and just being human with them.

4. The teacher must *listen.*

   The importance of listening means a respect for silence and offering help when necessary. It allows him or her to process and come up with his or her own answers.

5. The teacher must provide some *physical movement* during the day.

   Students need to move regularly during a school day. Middle and high school students change classes.

6. The teacher must be *aware.*

   A teacher is aware of feelings and prejudices. The classroom is a smaller version of the larger community, and issues can be played out and impact the class.

7. Other qualities that help build a successful classroom are:
   a. Honesty
   b. Unity
   c. Dealing with emotions
   d. Acceptance
   e. Respect — an important quality we have emphasized in this book.

The physical environment and atmosphere of the classroom are important to the overall success of effective teaching and student learning. Having your classroom ready and running when students come in the first day will help them adjust to the new sur-roundings, and they will know you care about them and their successes.

These are four main guidelines teachers need to consider about the learning space in the classroom. The following are effective suggestions for setting up a classroom.

1. Classroom environment
   a. Are materials accessible to students at all times?
   b. Are shelves and storage areas clear and organized?
   c. Are pathways clear of congestion? (pencil sharpener, trash cans, etc.)
   d. Are desks arrangements in a clear view of instructional areas?
2. Classroom atmosphere
   a. Is the teaching space open for contact with all students?
   b. Is the learning space available for small group and independent learning?
   c. Do you have space for materials that meet the curriculum?
3. Physical arrangement and learning problems
   a. Do you keep room temperatures comfortable?
   b. Are the instructional areas free from the hallway and other interferences?
   c. Do you have a retreat area for a student to complete independent work?
   d. Are you using colors, textures, plants,

posters, and decorated bulletin boards
to create a softness in the classroom?
4. Alter the classroom environment
    a. Are you personalizing the classroom
      space so it communicates the individu-
      ality of you and your students?
    b. Do you evaluate regularly and secure the
      classroom with safety standards for fire,
      earthquakes, and emergency situations?
    c. Do you secure equipment and materials
      with locks?

"When students feel safe, secure, and are engaged in the classroom educational process, and know the expectations, the classroom environment becomes positive and learning increases. Learning decreases when students feel threatened, unchallenged, and there is not a support system for regular learning successes."

—Marzano, et al, 1992

If you are promoting and maintaining high expectations, then the elements of a supportive classroom (comprehensive plans, vision, goals, objectives, a good classroom management program, clear communication, consistency, and celebrations of successes) will be visible to you and your students. Take the time to know your students by accessing prior knowledge and work habits. Students must be involved in the learning process and participate in the development and results of skills and instruction.

Believe in the Impossible:
A Flexible Classroom Curriculum

Introduction

Accomplished and successful teaching is not easy to define—and more difficult to achieve. Planning and creating a flexible curriculum that involves students in active learning and promotes diversity are ideals all teachers strive for in their strategic plans. What should all teachers know and be able to do?

1. Teachers are to be committed to a clear vision, goals, objectives, complete plans, and to students and their successes in learning.

   Am I committed to students and their learning?

   How am I evaluating the individuality of all students?

   Do I assess the student strengths and weaknesses for reviewing my lesson plans?

2. Teachers should know the subjects they teach and a variety of perspectives on teaching those subjects in a successful approach.

   Do students understand the content and skill areas?

   Do my teaching methods improve or create confusion for students?

   Is there a better way to teach a particular lesson? Do I consult other professionals?

3. Teachers are responsible to have a firm,

but fair, management program and assessment procedures for student learning and progress.

How do I assess student learning? Are they comprehensive?

Am I aware if each student has met the standards and expectations for the content?

4. Teachers should overplan for class and review methods and student progress. Take the time to learn from your experiences, other educators, and workshops.

Do I have a flexible curriculum to make changes to ensure effective learning?

What are areas for improvement so I am able to do better or become more effective?

5. Teachers are involved with other educators and members of learning communities.

What are some ways I share with other professionals?

How do I interact with other professionals to improve student learning?

Perspectives on Learning
(Auditory, Visual, and Kinesthetic)

Students need to learn and process information using all three styles of learning. A dominant learning approach defines the best way a person assimilates new information. The style may not always be the same for some tasks. The student may prefer one style for one task and a combination of others for a different task. Teachers must be prepared in their strategic plans to incorporate auditory, visual, and kinesthetic methods for all students and make an effort to match the instructional style for the student's learning strength. This is not always an easy task. Teachers have informed me over the years that visual presentations through the use of pictures and actual involvement in the learning process are advantageous for all students.

Auditory Learning

You will find auditory learners talk to themselves, move their lips, and read out loud. They may find some difficulty with reading and writing tasks. They are more successful talking and using a tape recorder.

1. Offer verbal explanations for what is coming, new material, and summaries.
2. Question learners orally to draw as much information as possible from students.
3. Increase auditory activities: brainstorming, small groups, and other verbal activities.
4. Have learners verbalize the questions.

Visual Learners

Learners who are "visual-linguistic" are successful through writing, in reference to reading and creative writing. They remember what is written and pay more attention to lectures if they watch them. Learners who are "visual-spatial" have difficulty with the written language and more success with videos, charts, and demonstrations. The imagination is a tool for them to become familiar with new surroundings.

1. Use the following visuals: charts, illustrations, maps, agendas, and handouts.
2. Include plenty of content in handouts to reread after class.
3. Leave space on handouts for notes.
4. Invite questions to help students stay alert.
5. Eliminate potential distractions.
6. Supplement text information with drawings, pictures, and role-playing.

Kinesthetic Learners

Kinesthetic learners do best by touching and moving. Students may lose concentration if there is little or no external stimulation or movement. When listening to a lecture, they may want to take notes to keep their hands moving. When reading, students like to scan the material and then focus on details using colored markers.

1. Use activities that give learners movement: music (when appropriate), colored markers to emphasize key points, frequent stretch breaks, use the five senses, and highlighters.
2. Guide learners through a visualization of complex tasks.
3. Have them transfer information from the text to another format: computer, tablet, notebook, chart, and map.

Perspective on Learning

Logical and Mathematical Learners

The description logical and mathematical learners refers to individuals and their ability to do things with data by collecting, organizing, analyzing, interpreting, concluding, and predicting. Teachers need to help students see patterns and relationships. Problem solving, playing strategy games, and solving mathematic problems are interests for these students.

1. Encourage computer usage and program languages and critical thinking activities.
2. Use real-life examples, science fiction scenarios, and logic puzzles for motivation.

Naturalistic Learners

Students who recognize and classify plants, animals, and minerals are naturalistic learners. They are able to evaluate specimens, value the unusual, and notice the natural and artificial in everyday life. Teachers can increase intelligence and interest by using relationships among species and classification activities.

1. Encourage the study of relationships such as patterns and order.
2. Assign compare-and-contrast activities to be aware of real-life and science issues.

Musical Learners

Musical intelligence refers to the ability to understand, create, and interpret all phases of music. Teachers can integrate activities into the lessons that encourage a student's musical intelligence by playing music for the class and creating lyrics about the material being taught.

Interpersonal Learners

Interpersonal learners have the ability to interpret and respond to moods, emotions, and actions of others. Interpersonal and intrapersonal intelligences find a lot of interplay between the two, and sometimes they are grouped together. Students would have good communication, interaction skills, and empathy toward the feelings of others. Teachers can design lessons that include cooperative group activities.

Intrapersonal Learners

Intrapersonal learners have the ability to know themselves and are aware of their own strengths and weaknesses. Teachers can help these students by assigning them journaling assignments.

Multiple Intelligences: Classroom Application
(Table by Brandy, Bellamy, and Camille Baker, 2005)

Verbal/Linguistic

> Teacher Centered
> + Present content verbally.
> + Ask questions aloud and look for student feedback.
> + Interviews

> Student Centered
> + Student presents material.
> + Students read content and prepare a presentation for classmates.
> +Students debate an issue.

Logical/Mathematical

> Teacher Centered
> + Provide brainteasers or challenging questions to begin lessons.
> + Make logical connections between the subject matter and authentic situations to answer the question "why?"

Student Centered
+ Students categorize information in logical sequences for organization.
+ Students create graphs or charts to explain written information.
+ Students participate in web quests associated with the content.

Bodily/Kinesthetic

Teacher Centered
+ Use props during lecture.
+ Provide tangible items pertaining to content for students to examine.
+ Review using sports related examples (throw a ball to someone to answer a question).

Student Centered
+ Students use computers to research subject matter.

+ Students create props of their own explaining subject matter (shadow boxes, mobiles, etc.).
+ Students create review games.

Visual/Spatial

Teacher Centered
+ When presenting the information, use visuals to explain content: PowerPoint,

slides, charts, graphs, cartoons, videos, overheads, and smartboards.

Student Centered
+ Have students work individually or in groups to create visuals pertaining to the information: posters, timelines, models, PowerPoint slides, maps, illustrations, charts, and concept mapping.

Musical

Teacher Centered
+ Play music in the classroom during reflective periods.
+ Show example or create musical rhythms for students to remember things.

Student Centered
+ Create a song or melody with the concept embedded for memory.
+ Use well-known songs to memorize formulas, skills, or test content.

Interpersonal

Teacher Centered
+ Be aware of body language and facial expressions.
+ Offer assistance whenever needed.
+ Encourage classroom discussion.

Student Centered
+ Encourage collaboration among peers.
+ Group work strengthens interpersonal connections.
+ Peer feedback and peer tutoring.
+ Students present to the class.

Intrapersonal

Teacher Centered
+ Encourage journaling as a positive outlet for expression.
+ Introduce web logging (blogs).
+ Make individual questions welcome.
+ Create a positive environment.

Student Centered
+ Journaling
+ Individual research on content
+ Students create personal portfolios of work.

Naturalistic

Teacher Centered
+ Take students outside to enjoy nature while in learning process (lecture).
+ Compare authentic subject matter to natural occurrences.
+ Relate subject matter to stages that occur in nature (plants, weather, etc.).

Student Centered

+ Students organize thoughts using natural cycles.

+ Students make relationships among content and the natural environment (how has nature had an impact?).

+ Students perform community service.

Planning a Flexible Classroom Curriculum

Student-centered lesson:

1. Identify clear goals, objectives, and outcomes.
2. Consider instructional activities that will utilize the multiple intelligences.
3. Allow students to explore materials that use multiple intelligences.
4. Assign a time frame for the lesson or unit.
5. Allow students to make decisions designing activities and tasks.
6. Design activities that are student-centered and use the inquiry models of learning.
7. Provide a rubric with students for activities.
8. Utilize assessment into the learning process.

Teacher-centered lesson:

1. Identify clear vision, goals, and instructional objectives.

2. Consider teacher-centered activities that relate to the multiple intelligences.
3. Plan what resources and materials are used for the lesson.
4. Specify a time frame for the lesson or unit.
5. Provide an opportunity for thinking and reflection.
6. Provide a rubric with students for activities.
7. Integrate assessment into the learning process.

Benefits of multiple intelligences:

1. Provide students with options and a variety of ways to learn.
2. Plan for all forms of intelligences.
3. Display student work to encourage more parent and community involvement.
4. Increase self-esteem, self-worth, and morale to increase student strengths.
5. Develop problem-solving skills to use in real-life situations.

Assessment

Organizing and planning to incorporate the multiple intelligence styles in lesson planning is not always an easy task for teachers. Assessment is one of the biggest challenges to include within strategic plans, along with the various intelligences. We all realize that assessment gives students the opportunity to demonstrate understanding of the skill or subject matter.

Teachers who guide students to use multiple intelligences styles along with an assessment process will help them to demonstrate their understanding of the material. Teachers need to make their goals, objectives, and expectations clear to students.

Achieve the Incredible:
A Success-Oriented
Classroom Atmosphere

Introduction

Achieve the incredible in your classroom by motivating student self-esteem and building morale. Self-esteem is simply an attitude we feel about ourselves and those qualities are self-confidence, self-acceptance, being positive, taking responsibility for one's actions, seeking challenges, and achieving goals.

Children who possess high self-esteem feel a sense of trust, security, and are accepted by others. Teachers need to recognize in building self-esteem and morale that it is important to create activities that are engaging. Allow students to make their own decisions, and offer praise for accomplishments when appropriate. Frustrating experiences are opportunities for growth and help students focus on problem-solving techniques. When children begin adolescence, self-esteem drops due to changes in the body and mind. Communication, listening, and understanding are all key qualities for reassuring the teenager as much as possible. Teachers are responsible for motivation as a key characteristic to reinforce self-esteem and morale in students and a class.

Regardless of the normal "ups and downs" of life, a teacher faces the physical, mental, and emotional changes of children and teenagers on a daily basis. Students with healthy or high self-esteem allow the "ups and downs" to temporarily limit them, while those with poor self-esteem see changes and challenges affecting their lives and making a difference.

When a child is growing up, their successes and failures are determined on how they are treated by family, teachers, coaches, religious authorities, and peers. The reality is our self-esteem develops and evolves throughout our lives through different people, goals we have reached, successes, decisions we make, and activities.

Getting to Know You

Name:_____   Date: _____

Answer all the survey statements and questions. Your answers will help me to get to know you better and make this a good year for you. This survey will be collected and kept privately.

Please Print

1. I am _____ years old and live in the city of _____
_____

2. My main cultural background is
   1. _____
   2. _____

3. I think it is important to be _____
    _____

4. I think I'm good at _____
    _____

5. I wish I could be better at _____
    _____

6. Three words that describe me are
    _____

7. My family thinks I should _____
    _____

8. I think I should _____
    _____

9. Sometimes I feel sad when _____
    _____

10. I collect _____
    _____

11. I speak these languages other than English:
    _____ I do not speak another language
    _____

12. I play the following musical instruments:

Instrument: _____
            _____

        How many years: _____
                        _____

What instruments to you play fairly well now?
    (Check or write)
    _____ piano _____ guitar _____ flute _____ clarinet
    _____trumpet _____ drums _____ violin
    Other: _____

13. I like to sing:
_____ yes   _____ no
_____ I would like to learn

14. I like to dance:
_____ yes   _____ no
_____ I would like to learn

15. My best subjects are:
    _____ Literature   _____ English
    _____ Math   _____ Vocabulary
    _____ Handwriting _____ Art
    _____ Social Studies_____ Science   _____ P.E.
    _____ Music   _____ Foreign language
    _____ Computer

16. My least favorite subjects are:
    _____ Literature   _____ English
    _____ Math   _____ Vocabulary
    _____ Handwriting _____ Art
    _____ Social Studies_____ Science_____ P. E.
    _____ Music   _____ Foreign language
    _____ Computer

17. Would you rather work with one partner, with a group of students, or by yourself?
    Check one: _____ one partner
    _____ with a group of students _____ by yourself

18. Do you feel more comfortable with one best friend or with a lot of friends?
    Check one: _____ one best friend
    _____ with lots of friends

19. What is something that is hard for you to do?

    _____

20. Somebody I really respect is

    _____
    _____

21. What do you like about school?

    _____

22. My best memory from summer is

    _____

23. How many books did you read this summer?
    _____ None   _____ 1
    _____ 2–4   _____ 5 or more

Form by Robert Grossi

Self-Esteem

Childhood experiences that lead to healthy self-esteem include:

1. Being praised
2. Being listened to
3. Being spoken to with respect
4. Getting attention and love
5. Experiencing success in school, sports, music, art
6. Having trustworthy friends

Childhood experiences that lead to low self-esteem include:

1. Being harshly criticized
2. Being yelled at, beaten, or put-down
3. Being ignored, ridiculed, or teased
4. Being expected to be "perfect" all the time
5. Experiencing failures in school and sports

Steps to Better Self-Esteem

If you want to improve your self-esteem, you must first believe that you can change it. Change takes time and doesn't happen quickly or easily. Once you have accepted or considered the possibility that you are not powerless, you will find these basic suggestions will boost yourself and your students' self-esteem.

Step one: Challenge the negative messages coming from your inner voice.

Scenario one:

"My friends said my oral report was good. But it wasn't that complete, and I messed up in so many places."

Better choice:

Cool! Everyone liked my report. It wasn't perfect, but I worked hard on my presentation and did a good job. I'm proud of myself."

Be reassuring with yourself.

Scenario two:

"I failed the test, and I don't understand anything in class. I'm so stupid."

Better choice:

"I did poorly on the test, but I've done okay on all the homework. There are some things here that I don't know as well as I thought I did, but I am going to review them and get help."

Be reassuring with yourself.

Scenario three:

"He is frowning and staring at me. He didn't say anything. It means he doesn't like me."

Better choice:

"He's frowning at me, and I don't know why; it could have nothing to do with me. Maybe I should ask.

Challenge the illogic of situations.

Scenario four:

"She turned me down for a date. I'm so embarrassed and humiliated. No one likes me or cares about me. I'll never find a girlfriend, and I'll always be alone."

Better choice:

"Whoa! That hurt! Well, she doesn't want to go out with me. That doesn't mean that no one does. I know I am an attractive and nice person. I will find someone."

Be *objective* about a situation.

Step two: Listening critically to your inner voice is the first step, but treating yourself as a worthwhile person enhances you as valuable, competent, deserving, and lovable.

1. Make it a habit to take care of yourself, physically and mentally.
2. Plan times for recreation and fun with friends.
3. Celebrate your accomplishments in and out of school.
4. Keep reminders of your strengths and achievements (awards, certificates, mementos).
5. Forgive yourself for mistakes, challenges, and not reaching specific expectations.

Watch your inner voice and avoid being overly critical.
6.   Be kind to yourself even though you don't feel you deserve it.

Step three: The most important step to improve self-esteem is to seek help, but it can also be the most difficult. Students and adults with low self-esteem aren't comfortable asking for help because they feel they don't deserve it. Parents and teachers, this is your opportunity to encourage positive action.

1.   Ask friends to share with you what they like about you.
2.   Ask family, friends, or someone else who cares about you, to just listen to you.
3.   Ask someone to remind you what they do when they are in a "down time."
4.   Go to a teacher, advisor, tutor, for help with school.
5.   Build self-confidence by taking a class (art, music, dance, swimming).
6.   Talking to a counselor will help you learn more about yourself and improve self-esteem.

Motivation

Students who are motivated to attend school, want to learn, and are engaged in their work are driven by these four goals: success (mastery), curiosity (understanding), originality (self-expression), and positive relationships (involvement with others). If you would ask both teachers and students what work would you find motivating, the response would be work that stimulated their curiosity, expressed creativity, and encouraged positive relationships.

Teachers I have interviewed have seen these qualities come to the surface during projects, presentations, role-playing, small-group work, and lively class discussions. As educators, we have our challenges and difficulties to find models and discover what our students want and need. We need to ask ourselves these questions:

1. Under what conditions and atmosphere are students most likely to be successful?
2. When are students most likely to become curious?
3. How can we help students satisfy their drive for self-expression?
4. How can we motivate a desire in students to learn and foster good peer relationships?

You have students in your classes that are naturally enthusiastic about learning, but many others need direction, challenge, and inspiration from the teacher. Your planning, vision, goals, objectives, management program, other teacher practices, and classroom ability will provide an interactive learning environment for students. Do you have a genuine interest in the students you are teaching?

Educators are aware there is no "magic wand" for motivating students, developing their self-esteem, and encouraging positive morale. Many reasons affect an individual student's motivation to work effectively and learn successfully: subject interest, how useful it is to them, desire to achieve, self-confidence, positive self-esteem, support, patience, persistence, and individual needs.

These are not new components for teachers, but they are great questions to brainstorm as you begin a new school year. I have used these and other educational questions to review at the beginning and middle of the school year: where I am as a teacher, where I need to be moving forward as a teacher, and how students are involved in the learning environment. These are questions for teachers.

1. Did you discover each student's inner needs and plan a successful curriculum?
2. How do you involve students in the learning process?
3. What ways do you guide students to be part of the class decision-making process?
4. Do you prepare realistic and challenging expectations for students?
5. Are you encouraging and helping students plan achievable goals to evaluate progress?
6. Are students clear on what they need to be successful in your class?

7. What lessons and activities strengthen self-esteem and morale?
8. Do students feel successful and have a sense of challenge with skills and content?
9. Do you offer a variety of teaching methods and activities?
10. Is the emphasis on learning and mastery of skills instead of grades?
11. Are you responding promptly to students with feedback on successes (self-esteem)?
12. How specific are comments given about weaknesses (avoid negative comments)?
13. What do you say to students about improvement and succeeding over time?
14. How do you share approaches to resolving problems (academic and personal)?
15. What ways do you recognize and reward sincere success when appropriate?

Character Building and Self-Esteem

School districts, schools, teachers, and parents everywhere are expressing a concern about the incorporation of character education instruction to be included in the overall curriculum from grades kindergarten through high school. There are too many students unaware of the basic character traits needed for successful living. The lack of role models and breakdown of their examples in society leave children few ways to learn correct character traits. Finding positive role models is not the only reason for the "downward swing" of character development. There is an increase in troubling youth trends and an overall moral decline: violence, vandalism, stealing, cheating, disrespect for authority, and other concerns.

A positive home life, with family and school working as a team may be the last hope for many students to understand and value the traits of responsibility, respect, caring, and cooperation. Teachers who are committed and caring have a chance to teach students solid character values. These character traits are taught as a separate subject or are integrated within the various subject areas. The best character lessons are ones that blend naturally into your existing lesson plans (literature, social studies, videos, music, news articles, and historical figures). Remember, you can achieve the incredible! The qualities of self-esteem and morale among students will produce confidence, interest, respect, and leadership.

Everyone at the school site reinforces and models the same trait to provide opportunities for students to learn and practice it. Posters, an assembly, screen savers, and weekly announcements are suggestions.

Prepare lessons plans and convey to students the meaning of character traits and why they are important to learn. It is vital to provide real ways and experiences students can practice these traits. Literature, news articles, discussions, brainstorming, and oral presentations will help demonstrate the value and meaning of the traits.

Teach the new trait as a skill, and tell students how to behave, demonstrate, and observe the trait in action. If you model the character trait and make your lessons as concrete as possible, it will make it real in his or her life. Employ role-playing, skits, and photographs of others modeling a trait so they are reminded of what the skill looks like.

Provide and arrange frequent opportunities for students to practice the trait. When planning activities, it takes twenty-one days of practice to acquire a new behavior. Videotapes, journals, assignments, and homework are ways to practice the trait.

Offer effective feedback to reinforce appropriate behavior and correct any bad habits. It is important to consistently clarify and guide students: "You're on the right track," "What you did was not right, but this is what you can do next," or, "Catch students doing the trait right."

Summary: Part Three

The title of this book is See! Believe! Achieve! What an intriguing goal for all teachers and educators to inspire and connect with students. The "heart and soul" of teaching is yourself as a person, including knowledge, attitude, motivation, planning, interest in students, and self-growth - both personally and academically.

See! Believe! Achieve! becoming a reality involves teachers creating an environment of success for each student in their classrooms. What a task! Not impossible, and achievements by students can be incredible.

You are already aware of the words *coach* or *coaching*, and they remind you of sports. A coach guides the team to a success. Coaching is very appropriate for describing the functions of educators who lead students to knowledge and truth through discussion and problem solving. It is a continuous process providing students with feedback, observing performance, offering feedback, and helping them to develop thinking skills. There are a few teaching strategies that are common to the "coaching" style of educating students: instruction or retraining, directing or guiding, and encouragement. Your strategic plans should gear for a success-oriented and successful environment for all students.

Believe in the Impossible means there is flexibility in your classroom curriculum promoting diversity and a variety of perspectives on learning. Being aware of the diverse groups of students in your classroom offers the reality that all people are unique in their own way. Differences may include reading level, athletic ability, musical or artistic talents, cultural background, personality, religious beliefs, and I could go on. Teachers should value diversity and model the attitude to students. Example: When attempting to solve a problem, it is best to assemble diverse student teams to approach many skills and different ways to resolve the situation. Teachers who plan flexibility in their classroom curriculum provide an environment that is conducive to learning, and this makes an atmosphere open for a variety of perspectives on learning.

Achieve the Incredible is possible if every teacher continually offers the students hope. Hope changes perception of each student's view of himself or herself. Hope helps students get through the difficult days and move forward on better ones. Hope reminds them of healing from hurts and gives confidence for the future. These aren't new concepts; they are visible in each classroom. All students have something they are good at, and an investment of time and energy in developing a talent or ability will become a strength. Teachers may be the only ones in a student's life to shine a light of awareness of gifts.

"Most folks are about as happy as they make up their minds to be." (Abraham Lincoln)

Our positive attitudes are built from feedback from parents, friends, teachers, society, and self that forms our own self-image and world-image. Be alert to changing attitudes through your inner voice and conversation. Commitment, control, and challenge help build self-esteem and promote positive thinking.

Teachers are instrumental in helping students *Achieve the Incredible* by making them develop a positive commitment to learning, working together on goals and objectives, reinforcing strategies for dealing with problems, accepting challenges, and by showing them how to be courageous and how to relax and enjoy successes.

Part Four

See the Invisible, Believe in the Impossible, and Achieve the Incredible

Section One: What Is Your Road Map to Teaching and Planning?

Step One: Pre-Planning Considerations

1. Vision: Write a description of your classroom instructional plan.
2. Mission Statement: "Where will we be in five years?" (relates to vision and school values)
3. Goals: These are broad statements and are measurable.
4. Objectives: Objectives are specific and measurable statements (achievement of goals).
5. Philosophy: Philosophy are ideas and beliefs by teachers, the school, and the district.
6. Outcomes: Outcomes are attitude changes, knowledge, behavior, and skills with students.

Step Two: Organization and Decision-Making

Good thinking + Organization + Decision-making = Good teaching! The wisdom and freedom to create a classroom instructional program that includes discoveries, success-oriented lessons and activities, and involves students in the learning process is an invaluable resource.

Step Three: Lesson Planning

Do you recall the story about the frog and beautiful young maiden? The moral of the story was that teachers are to kiss as many frogs as possible! Your long-term, short-term, and daily plans are key to turning those frogs into young princes and princesses. Always be prepared with your alternate plans and "bag of tricks."

Step Four: Assessment

Authentic and performance assessment are tools for effective feedback for teachers and students. Teachers need to realize that these are goals for improvement in student learning and feedback for instructional successes. Never pass up the opportunity and time for self-evaluation and reflection of daily lesson successes and needs.

Step Five: Classroom Management

You are the positive force, as a teacher, to ensure students experience successes as students and individuals. They must understand what positive behavior is, enjoy positive behavior, and practice positive behavior. The goal of discipline is to create opportunities for students to develop self-discipline; thereby, they are involved in the overall learning process of the curriculum. Teachers who provide an interesting instructional program, active learning environment, and work with students on developing self-discipline and responsibility have a higher success rate with positive behavior with students.

Step Six: See the Invisible

See the invisible and possibilities for a solid education for students in a supportive environment. What are the results of effective planning and a success-oriented instruction for you and your students?

Step Seven: Believe in the Impossible

Yes, you do believe in the impossible! Then, as a teacher, you are the motivator to use your talents and planning instruments as a collaborative approach to identify and know your students' gifts. Affirming each student's gifts is a motivating force to call them for participation in the learning environment.

Step Eight: Achieve the Incredible

Your modeling and leading the way offers students the example that you are committed to your vision and you practice what you preach. What are your values (morale)? Do you help students see the bigger picture (self-esteem)? Are you consistently helping students manage their time well (social success)? Successes will build perceptions of capability and productive individuals, so emphasize self-esteem and morale building.

Section Two: Testimonies from Professional Educators

I sent a request for teacher friends and fellow educators to complete a survey and select three questions from a choice of eight. It was my goal to have each one share the "heart and soul" of teaching and how they connect with students. These are the questions:

1. Why did you want to be a teacher?
2. What parts of teaching appeal most to you? What parts appeal least?
3. What has been your most inspiring moment in teaching?
4. What do you think is the most challenging aspects of teaching?
5. How would you set up your classroom?
6. What types of assessments have you used?
7. Why is short and long-range planning so important?
8. How do you involve students in the learning process?

• • • • • • • • • • • • •

Cathy Bradshaw

Grades sixth, seventh, eighth, and high school; language arts and social studies

1. My classroom environment was always important. I was very conscious of proper air, light, and temperature. More, I real-

219

ized that for many students the classroom was their place of order, security, and safety. The classroom needed to reflect respect each student was due. The room was clean and the floors clear. Each month the color scheme and decorations were changed. During the day when there was no formal instruction, classical music was played.

2. The most inspiring event in my teaching career occurred after it ended. One of my students from twenty years back set out to find me. He even contacted the bishop in his search. Well, we did connect, and he wanted to let me know that a "lecture" I had given him when he was in my seventh grade had made all the difference in his life. He had to thank me before his life on this earth ended. He was dying of cancer. He died a few months after we met. I remember the lecture, the need for it, and am positive it was divinely inspired. Teachers need to listen too.

3. The hardest part of teaching today is the lack of support from teaching. Parents often pass their roles to teachers and then find fault in their child's education when the child fails to succeed due to lack of sleep, proper food, and reinforcement at home. The local school community has little to say in a child's welfare. The state government on the advice of "experts" places unreal and unnatural expectations on stu-

dents. The federal government is using schools to propel education in the wrong directions. We need to get back to a safe, respectful, and responsible school environment for both students and teachers.

Charles Denton

Grades seventh and eighth; math and science

1. Teaching is a noble profession. I like to help students through math and science to search for their place in life. It is my hope that each child fits in society and finds their purpose in life.
2. My most inspiring moment is when I see my students setting goals, writing them down, and how they plan to achieve them. I guide them in the process. When there is a sense of accomplishment, it permeates their entire life.
3. Teaching becomes challenging when I make an effort to overcome obstacles that I am really committed to do something important.

Maria Rodriguez

Grades first through fourth

1. In kindergarten, after what seemed like endless hours, I could hardly wait to go

home and play school with my imaginary friend, Johnny! When I found myself in the world of fantasy, I actually taught him to speak English clearly. Johnny became my avenue to teaching—I knew I could do it. Teach, but be a good teacher so I may touch the lives of young minds with love and understanding; a way that I didn't experience. I've always wanted to give kids the opportunity and the help (I didn't get) to learn and to succeed.

2. There have been many inspiring moments in my almost forty years of teaching, in private school, high school, public school, and adult school. But recently in my third grade class, this one student, who has only been in my class for four and a half months, has been inspirational, making teaching worthwhile. He suffered trauma and has emotional issues. One day he came quietly to me with a drawing addressed: "To my teacher Mrs. R (me)." He gave me the drawing, a big smile on his face. I thanked him. When I shared this with the principal, I was told that this student had made a connection with me; a rare thing. I had reached him! It's moments like this that have kept me teaching. These moments are worth millions.

3. The most challenging aspect of teaching is a new class every school year. This is the area of the unknown. Every year I ask

myself: Where do I start? I have to plan accordingly to go with age, level, and rate of learning for my new class. I have to plan so my practice motivates and challenges all learners and keeps them safe. I set expectations so my students experience confidence and success in their learning. Teaching is hard. I love it!

Tanya

Grades third through fifth

1. I chose to be a teacher because, in addition to enjoying the experience of working with children, I am certain that it is the profession that God chose for me. Working with children of various ages has allowed me to make a positive difference in the world. Ironically, I did not imagine that I would be a teacher. My mother worked as a teacher for at least thirty years, and she was the world's most amazing teacher. She was incredibly committed to the practice. I was amazed when I found myself following in her path.

2. That which appeals to me is the same that I find inspiring. I cannot nail my most inspiring moment to a singular event, lest I do disservice to any of God's miracles. I am always inspired by a child who makes a sincere effort to do their best. It nearly

overwhelms me when a child succeeds at something that they thought they could not. It is also thrilling when students have "aha" moments; that "click" that happens when they understand something.

3. I find both short-range and long-range planning important. Long-range planning is important because one needs to know where they are guiding their students to go. In other words, what is the ultimate goal? Short-range planning (and may I add flexibility and spontaneity) are urgent because one must meet the students where they are, no matter where it is the teacher plans for them to go. Short-range planning is important in order to allow for unique opportunities as well as to meet the needs of individual students. Teachers must take into account school events and the like in their planning.

Robert Bradshaw

Grades ninth through twelfth

1. I find some of the most challenging moments to be having students and parents and teachers on the same page. I have found it enormously difficult in the last few years to get parents to be appropriately involved and supportive of their children's academic education. I have also found it challenging to secure necessary services for students in

need. I have also found myself concerned with the fact that it is sometimes difficult to help students develop their individual gifts, as they may be outside the realm of regular academics. There is also the personal demand upon teachers. Teachers work well beyond the scheduled school hours. They work as counselors, surrogate parents, disciplinarians, and sometimes dieticians. The "No Child Left Behind" has actually meant "A Lot of Teachers Left Behind!" Testing, testing.

2. Since learning is an individual process, the instructor cannot do it for the student. The student can learn only from personal experiences; therefore, my strategic plans involve students in auditory, visual, kinesthetic, and other styles of learning and knowledge that cannot exist apart from a person. A person's knowledge is a result of experience, and no two people have had identical experiences.

3. It is important to use more than one way to look at student assessment. Multiple sources give information from different perspectives. I use a variety of these techniques, and that creates an assessment "system" that is not rigid, but systematic in its processes and results. I ask probing questions of students, which has partially replaced giving directions. For example, when my students say they cannot figure out what to do next, I might ask, "What have you tried so far?"

"Tell me about your thinking," or, "What are some things you could try?" It gives me a better idea of helping students become more self-directing. Students will begin to ask themselves, "What else can we try?" I back observations and conversations with documentation, and it helps my lesson plans.

Section Three:
What Is the Future of Education, Teaching, and Student Learning?

Where will you be in the next ten or twenty years as an educator? Can you imagine a school without desks or walls? What do you see as the classroom of the future? Technological developments will be so common and found in homes, businesses, and schools. At this point in time, and in perfecting educational training and student learning techniques, there is not a clear road map.

1. The integration of computers, television, and telecommunications are seen through digital techniques. There also will be more use of laptops in the classroom.
2. There will be reduced costs for fiber optics and cellular communication devices.
3. An increased processing power in a smaller container will be available through microchip and advanced software techniques.
4. There will be an integration of entertainment/communication, purchasing, and education through television programs, music, home shopping, banking, classes, and training.

In modern learning theory there will possibly be several educational goals for meaning and relevance as securing knowledge for life skills. Learning is as much a social as an individual activity. A key principle of the classroom for the future is providing teachers the necessary technological, professional development that helps them change teaching practices. Teachers will be facilitators, guides, and coinvestigators, and students will be the producers, apprentices, and coexplorers of knowledge and information.

High schools will be focusing and expanding critical learning skills and creating relevant and personalized information environments to ensure success of students in the world. High school students are destined to enter the work force and life in an increasingly competitive world of seeking jobs and higher education. Educators are responsible for making these realizations a success for students. What would be some possibilities for improvement in teaching and learning in English, math, science, and social studies?

1. English
   a. Develop websites to support advanced research skills, make digital movies, compose songs, and write narrative essays.
   b. Observe Martin Luther King delivering his "I Have a Dream" speech, and write a presentation on how it would affect a group of people today.

2. Math
   a. Design and construct virtual models.

   b. Create a virtual universe using an online Hubble telescope to investigate stars.

3. Science
   a. Students may go on a NASA or JPL Mission to analyze jet propulsion forces, or examine the stars or a meteorite.
   b. Travel underwater to discover sunken treasures of lost civilizations, and observe different species of fish through a video on a research ship.

4. Social Studies
   a. Develop a Web site or investigate a Weblog to identify the causes of World War II, and make a multimedia presentation.
   b. Examine artifacts, and engage in discussions with anthropologists about the culture of various societies.

Sometimes, there are books we have read or movies we have watched or experiences we've had as children that can be recalled with greater meaning as we mature and become older. There is a passage in Margery William's book, *The Velveteen Rabbit*, which has this beautiful power to help us think and grow.

Briefly, this story tells us about a little toy rabbit, first well-loved, then ignored by the boy who receives it as a Christmas gift. The rabbit is saddened to be cast aside and seeks the wisdom of an older, worn-out toy, the Skin Horse. The Velveteen Rabbit is really seeking what all humans want: *Acceptance*! But he asks instead, "What is it like being "real"?

> "What is real?" asked the rabbit one day, as they were lying side by side. "Does it mean having things that buzz inside you, and a stick out handle?"
>
> "Real isn't how you're made," said the skin horse. "It's a thing that happens to you. When a child loves you for a long, long time—not just to play with—but really loves you—then you become real."
>
> "Does it hurt?" asked the rabbit.
>
> "Sometimes," said the skin horse, for he always spoke the truth. "When you are real, you don't mind being hurt."
>
> "Does it happen all at once, like being wound up, or little by little?"
>
> "It doesn't happen all at once. You just become! It takes a long time. That's why it doesn't often happen to people who break easily, or have sharp edges, or have to be carefully kept. Generally, by the time you are real, most of your hair has been rubbed off and your eyes drop out, and you become loose at the joints and very shabby."

As we put away childish thoughts and move forward to new beginnings, let us not forget those real moments of growth and understanding as a child, adult, and teacher. We appreciate our many blessings and take courage in the gifts of new possibilities.

Teachers and fellow educators, challenge your teaching journey with a road map of thoughts, attitudes, "tried and true" methods, materials, and teacher involvement tips for classroom planning. Turn those frogs into young princesses and princes able to handle the realities of life. Teachers, you have the power to develop those gifts in students.

We have the ability to aid one another through difficult times and to understand each other.

We should develop a strong sense of faith in each other and learn to work individually and in unity at any time. Hope means never ceasing to be amazed, wearing your soul on your sleeve, holding your breath, waiting to hear, "I love you, too," but most of all believing that you'll make a difference and that you matter. Yes, the "heart and soul" of education and learning is both for students and teachers.

So, the lights of success are turned on. You have found the "best way" to teach, and your goals, organization, planning, environment, curriculum, and collaboration with students are ready—so, best wishes, and continue to *see the invisible, believe in the impossible, and achieve the incredible.*